Sigrid Estrada

Barbara Ehrenreich is the author of sixteen previous
books, including the bestsellers *Nickel and Dimed* and
Bait and Switch. A frequent contributor to *Harper's*
and *The Nation,* she has also been a columnist at *The
New York Times* and *Time* magazine.

www.barbaraehrenreich.com

Also by Barbara Ehrenreich

This Land Is Their Land: Reports from a Divided Nation

Dancing in the Streets: A History of Collective Joy

Bait and Switch: The (Futile) Pursuit of the American Dream

Nickel and Dimed: On (Not) Getting By in America

Blood Rites: Origins and History of the Passions of War

The Snarling Citizen

Kipper's Game

The Worst Years of Our Lives:
Irreverent Notes from a Decade of Greed

Fear of Falling: The Inner Life of the Middle Class

The Hearts of Men:
American Dreams and the Flight from Commitment

Global Woman:
Nannies, Maids, and Sex Workers in the New Economy
(with Arlie Russell Hochschild)

Re-making Love: The Feminization of Sex
(with Elizabeth Hess and Gloria Jacobs)

For Her Own Good: 150 Years of the Experts' Advice to Women
(with Deirdre English)

Witches, Midwives, and Nurses: A History of Women Healers
(with Deirdre English)

Complaints and Disorders: The Sexual Politics of Sickness
(with Deirdre English)

The Mean Season: The Attack on the Welfare State
(with Fred Block, Richard A. Cloward, and Frances Fox Piven)

Additional Praise for *Bright-Sided*

"A precisely crafted, hard-hitting . . . analysis of the national mass fantasy of wishful thinking."   —*The Dallas Morning News*

"Insightful, smart, and witty . . . Ehrenreich makes important points about what happens to those who dare to warn of the worst."
—*BusinessWeek*

"Relentless and persuasive . . . In a voice urgent and passionate, Ehrenreich offers us neither extreme [positive thinking nor being a spoilsport] but instead balance: joy, happiness, yes; sadness, anger, yes. She favors life with a clear head, eyes wide open. . . . *Bright-Sided* offers a surefire cure."   —*San Francisco Chronicle*

"Barbara Ehrenreich's study of American optimism at its most delusional is fascinating, often very funny, and wholly convincing. . . . As a portrait of America's desperate insistence on facile optimism, *Bright-Sided* is stunningly good . . . a highly entertaining, alarming read, and a ringing clarion call to America to brace up and remember Sod's law."   —*The Sunday Times* (UK)

"Ehrenreich convinced me completely. . . . I hesitate to say anything so positive as that this book will change the way you see absolutely everything; but it just might."   —*The Daily Beast*

"A sharp, funny critique."   —*People*

"Unless you keep on saying that you believe in fairies, Tinker Bell will check out, and what's more, her sad demise will be your fault! Barbara Ehrenreich scores again for the independent-minded in resisting this drool and all those who wallow in it."
—Christopher Hitchens, author of *God Is Not Great: How Religion Poisons Everything*

"Ehrenreich reprises her role as Dorothy swishing back the curtain on a great and powerful given." —*The Oregonian*

"A rousing endorsement of skepticism, realism, and critical thinking." —*San Francisco Bay Guardian*

"We're always being told that looking on the bright side is good for us, but now we see that it's a great way to brush off poverty, disease, and unemployment, to rationalize an order where all the rewards go to those on top. The people who are sick or jobless— why, they just aren't thinking positively. They have no one to blame but themselves. Barbara Ehrenreich has put the menace of positive thinking under the microscope. Anyone who's ever been told to brighten up needs to read this book."
—Thomas Frank, author of *The Wrecking Crew* and *What's the Matter with Kansas?*

"A message that deserves to be heard." —*Jezebel*

"Gleefully pops the positive-thinking bubble . . . Amazingly, she'll make you laugh, albeit ruefully, as she presents how society's relentless focus on being upbeat has eroded our ability to ask—and heed—the kind of uncomfortable questions that could have fended off economic disaster." —*FastCompany.com*

"A measured and informed attack on the 'cult of positive thinking' that first infected the United States and then spread to the rest of the world . . . The real value of Ehrenreich's book is that it shows that the choice is not between being positive or negative. The issue, according to Ehrenreich, is whether we start with the facts or with our attitudes." —*Financial Times* (UK)

"In this hilarious and devastating critique, Barbara Ehrenreich applies some much-needed negativity to the zillion-dollar business of positive thinking. This is truly a text for the times."
—Katha Pollitt, author of *The Mind-Body Problem: Poems*

BRIGHT-SIDED

BRIGHT-SIDED

How Positive Thinking

Is Undermining America

Barbara Ehrenreich

Picador

A Metropolitan Book
Henry Holt and Company
New York

www.picadorusa.com

Picador® is a U.S. registered trademark and is used by Henry Holt and
Company under license from Pan Books Limited.

For information on Picador Reading Group Guides, please contact Picador.
E-mail: readinggroupguides@picadorusa.com

The Library of Congress has cataloged the Henry Holt edition as follows:

Ehrenreich, Barbara.
  Bright-sided : how the relentless promotion of positive thinking has undermined
America / Barbara Ehrenreich.—1st ed.
      p.   cm.
  Includes bibliographical references and index.
  ISBN 978-0-8050-8749-9
  1. Optimism—United States.   2. Happiness—United States.   3. Self-confidence—
United States.   4. Success in business—United States.   I. Title.
  BF698.35.O57E37 2009
  155.2'32—dc22

                                                                    2009023588

Picador ISBN 978-0-312-65885-4

First published in the United States by Henry Holt and Company

First Picador Edition: August 2010

10 9 8 7 6 5

To complainers everywhere:
Turn up the volume!

Contents

BRIGHT-SIDED

Introduction

Americans are a "positive" people. This is our reputation as well as our self-image. We smile a lot and are often baffled when people from other cultures do not return the favor. In the well-worn stereotype, we are upbeat, cheerful, optimistic, and shallow, while foreigners are likely to be subtle, world-weary, and possibly decadent. American expatriate writers like Henry James and James Baldwin wrestled with and occasionally reinforced this stereotype, which I once encountered in the 1980s in the form of a remark by Soviet émigré poet Joseph Brodsky to the effect that the problem with Americans is that they have "never known suffering." (Apparently he didn't know who had invented the blues.) Whether we Americans see it as an embarrassment or a point of pride, being positive—in affect, in mood, in outlook—seems to be engrained in our national character.

Who would be churlish or disaffected enough to challenge these happy features of the American personality? Take the business of positive "affect," which refers to the mood we display to others through our smiles, our greetings, our professions of confidence and optimism. Scientists have found that the mere act of smiling can generate positive feelings within us, at least if the smile is not forced. In addition, good feelings, as expressed through our words and smiles, seem to be contagious: "Smile and the world smiles with you." Surely the world would be a better, happier place if we all greeted one another warmly and stopped to coax smiles from babies—if only through the well-known social psychological mechanism of "mood contagion." Recent studies show that happy feelings flit easily through social networks, so that one person's good fortune can brighten the day even for only distantly connected others.[1]

Furthermore, psychologists today agree that positive feelings like gratitude, contentment, and self-confidence can actually lengthen our lives and improve our health. Some of these claims are exaggerated, as we shall see, though positive feelings hardly need to be justified, like exercise or vitamin supplements, as part of a healthy lifestyle. People who report having positive feelings are more likely to participate in a rich social life, and vice versa, and social connectedness turns out to be an important defense against depression, which is a known risk factor for many physical illnesses. At the risk of redundancy or even tautology, we can say that on many levels, individual and social, it is *good* to be "positive," certainly better than being withdrawn, aggrieved, or chronically sad.

So I take it as a sign of progress that, in just the last decade or so, economists have begun to show an interest in using happiness rather than just the gross national product as a measure of an economy's success. Happiness is, of course, a slippery thing to measure or define. Philosophers have debated what it is for centuries, and even if we were to define it simply as a greater frequency of positive feelings than negative ones, when we ask people if they are happy we are asking them to arrive at some sort of average over many moods and moments. Maybe I was upset earlier in the day but then was cheered up by a bit of good news, so what am I really? In one well-known psychological experiment, subjects were asked to answer a questionnaire on life satisfaction—but only after they had performed the apparently irrelevant task of photocopying a sheet of paper for the experimenter. For a randomly chosen half of the subjects, a dime had been left for them to find on the copy machine. As two economists summarize the results, "Reported satisfaction with life was raised substantially by the discovery of the coin on the copy machine—clearly not an income effect."[2]

In addition to the problems of measurement, there are cultural differences in how happiness is regarded and whether it is even seen as a virtue. Some cultures, like our own, value the positive affect that seems to signal internal happiness; others are more impressed by seriousness, self-sacrifice, or a quiet willingness to cooperate. However hard to pin down, though, happiness is somehow a more pertinent metric for well-being, from a humanistic perspective, than the buzz of transactions that constitute the GDP.

Surprisingly, when psychologists undertake to measure the relative happiness of nations, they routinely find that Americans are not, even in prosperous times and despite our vaunted positivity, very happy at all. A recent meta-analysis of over a hundred studies of self-reported happiness worldwide found Americans ranking only twenty-third, surpassed by the Dutch, the Danes, the Malaysians, the Bahamians, the Austrians, and even the supposedly dour Finns.[3] In another potential sign of relative distress, Americans account for two-thirds of the global market for antidepressants, which happen also to be the most commonly prescribed drugs in the United States. To my knowledge, no one knows how antidepressant use affects people's responses to happiness surveys: do respondents report being happy because the drugs make them feel happy or do they report being unhappy because they know they are dependent on drugs to make them feel better? Without our heavy use of antidepressants, Americans would likely rank far lower in the happiness rankings than we currently do.

When economists attempt to rank nations more objectively in terms of "well-being," taking into account such factors as health, environmental sustainability, and the possibility of upward mobility, the United States does even more poorly than it does when only the subjective state of "happiness" is measured. The Happy Planet Index, to give just one example, locates us at 150th among the world's nations.[4]

How can we be so surpassingly "positive" in self-image and stereotype without being the world's happiest and best-off people? The answer, I think, is that positivity is not so much our condition or our mood as it is part of our ideology—the way we explain the world and think we ought to function within it. That ideology is "positive thinking," by which we usually mean two things. One is the generic content of positive thinking—that is, the positive thought itself—which can be summarized as: Things are pretty good right now, at least if you are willing to see silver linings, make lemonade out of lemons, etc., and things are going to get a whole lot better. This is optimism, and it is not the same as hope. Hope is an emotion, a yearning, the experience of which is not entirely within our control. Optimism is a cognitive stance, a conscious expectation, which presumably anyone can develop through practice.

The second thing we mean by "positive thinking" is this practice, or discipline, of trying to think in a positive way. There is, we are told, a practical reason for undertaking this effort: positive thinking supposedly not only makes us feel optimistic but actually makes happy outcomes more likely. If you expect things to get better, they will. How can the mere process of thinking do this? In the rational explanation that many psychologists would offer today, optimism improves health, personal efficacy, confidence, and resilience, making it easier for us to accomplish our goals. A far less rational theory also runs rampant in American ideology—the idea that our thoughts can, in some mysterious way, directly affect the physical world. Negative thoughts somehow produce negative outcomes, while positive thoughts realize themselves in the form of health, prosperity, and success. For both rational and mystical reasons, then, the effort of positive thinking is said to be well worth our time and attention, whether this means reading the relevant books, attending seminars and speeches that offer the appropriate mental training, or just doing the solitary work of concentration on desired outcomes—a better job, an attractive mate, world peace.

There is an anxiety, as you can see, right here in the heart of American positive thinking. If the generic "positive thought" is correct and things are really getting better, if the arc of the universe tends toward happiness and abundance, then why bother with the mental effort of positive thinking? Obviously, because we do not fully believe that things will get better on their own. The practice of positive thinking is an effort to pump up this belief in the face of much contradictory evidence. Those who set themselves up as instructors in the discipline of positive thinking— coaches, preachers, and gurus of various sorts—have described this effort with terms like "self-hypnosis," "mind control," and "thought control." In other words, it requires deliberate self-deception, including a constant effort to repress or block out unpleasant possibilities and "negative" thoughts. The truly self-confident, or those who have in some way made their peace with the world and their destiny within it, do not need to expend effort censoring or otherwise controlling their thoughts. Positive thinking may be a quintessentially American activity, associated in our minds with both individual and national success, but it is driven by a terrible insecurity.

Americans did not start out as positive thinkers—at least the promotion of unwarranted optimism and methods to achieve it did not really find articulation and organized form until several decades after the founding of the republic. In the Declaration of Independence, the founding fathers pledged to one another "our lives, our fortunes, and our sacred honor." They knew that they had no certainty of winning a war for independence and that they were taking a mortal risk. Just the act of signing the declaration made them all traitors to the crown, and treason was a crime punishable by execution. Many of them did go on to lose their lives, loved ones, and fortunes in the war. The point is, they fought anyway. There is a vast difference between positive thinking and existential courage.

Systematic positive thinking began, in the nineteenth century, among a diverse and fascinating collection of philosophers, mystics, lay healers, and middle-class women. By the twentieth century, though, it had gone mainstream, gaining purchase within such powerful belief systems as nationalism and also doing its best to make itself indispensable to capitalism. We don't usually talk about American nationalism, but it is a mark of how deep it runs that we apply the word "nationalism" to Serbs, Russians, and others, while believing ourselves to possess a uniquely superior version called "patriotism." A central tenet of American nationalism has been the belief that the United States is "the greatest nation on earth"—more dynamic, democratic, and prosperous than any other nation, as well as technologically superior. Major religious leaders, especially on the Christian right, buttress this conceit with the notion that Americans are God's chosen people and that America is the designated leader of the world—an idea that seemed to find vivid reinforcement in the fall of Communism and our emergence as the world's "lone superpower." That acute British observer Godfrey Hodgson has written that the American sense of exceptionalism, which once was "idealistic and generous, if somewhat solipsistic," has become "harder, more hubristic." Paul Krugman responded to the prevailing smugness in a 1998 essay entitled "American the Boastful," warning that "if pride goeth before a fall, the United States has one heck of a come-uppance in store."[5]

But of course it takes the effort of positive thinking to imagine that America is the "best" or the "greatest." Militarily, yes, we are the mightiest nation on earth. But on many other fronts, the American score is dismal, and was dismal even before the economic downturn that began in 2007. Our children routinely turn out to be more ignorant of basic subjects like math and geography than their counterparts in other industrialized nations. They are also more likely to die in infancy or grow up in poverty. Almost everyone acknowledges that our health care system is "broken" and our physical infrastructure crumbling. We have lost so much of our edge in science and technology that American companies have even begun to outsource their research and development efforts. Worse, some of the measures by which we do lead the world should inspire embarrassment rather than pride: We have the highest percentage of our population incarcerated, and the greatest level of inequality in wealth and income. We are plagued by gun violence and racked by personal debt.

While positive thinking has reinforced and found reinforcement in American national pride, it has also entered into a kind of symbiotic relationship with American capitalism. There is no natural, innate affinity between capitalism and positive thinking. In fact, one of the classics of sociology, Max Weber's *Protestant Ethic and the Spirit of Capitalism*, makes a still impressive case for capitalism's roots in the grim and punitive outlook of Calvinist Protestantism, which required people to defer gratification and resist all pleasurable temptations in favor of hard work and the accumulation of wealth.

But if early capitalism was inhospitable to positive thinking, "late" capitalism, or consumer capitalism, is far more congenial, depending as it does on the individual's hunger for *more* and the firm's imperative of *growth*. The consumer culture encourages individuals to want more—cars, larger homes, television sets, cell phones, gadgets of all kinds—and positive thinking is ready at hand to tell them they deserve more and can have it if they really want it and are willing to make the effort to get it. Meanwhile, in a competitive business world, the companies that manufacture these goods and provide the paychecks that purchase them have no alternative but to grow. If you don't steadily increase market share and profits, you risk being driven out of business or swallowed by a larger enterprise. Perpetual growth, whether of a particular company or an entire economy, is of course an absurdity, but positive thinking makes it seem possible, if not ordained.

In addition, positive thinking has made itself useful as an apology for the crueler aspects of the market economy. If optimism is the key to material success, and if you can achieve an optimistic outlook through the discipline of positive thinking, then there is no excuse for failure. The flip side of positivity is thus a harsh insistence on personal responsibility: if your business fails or your job is eliminated, it must because you didn't try hard enough, didn't believe firmly enough in the inevitability of your success. As the economy has brought more layoffs and financial

turbulence to the middle class, the promoters of positive thinking have increasingly emphasized this negative judgment: to be
disappointed, resentful, or downcast is to be a "victim" and a
"whiner."

But positive thinking is not only a water carrier for the business world, excusing its excesses and masking its follies. The promotion of positive thinking has become a minor industry in its
own right, producing an endless flow of books, DVDs, and other
products; providing employment for tens of thousands of "life
coaches," "executive coaches," and motivational speakers, as well
as for the growing cadre of professional psychologists who seek
to train them. No doubt the growing financial insecurity of the
middle class contributes to the demand for these products and
services, but I hesitate to attribute the commercial success of positive thinking to any particular economic trend or twist of the
business cycle. America has historically offered space for all sorts
of sects, cults, faith healers, and purveyors of snake oil, and those
that are profitable, like positive thinking, tend to flourish.

At the turn of the twenty-first century, American optimism
seemed to reach a manic crescendo. In his final State of Union
address in 2000, Bill Clinton struck a triumphal note, proclaiming
that "never before has our nation enjoyed, at once, so much prosperity and social progress with so little internal crisis and so few
external threats." But compared with his successor, Clinton seemed
almost morose. George W. Bush had been a cheerleader in prep
school, and cheerleading—a distinctly American innovation—
could be considered the athletically inclined ancestor of so much
of the coaching and "motivating" that has gone into the propaga-
tion of positive thinking. He took the presidency as an opportunity to continue in that line of work, defining his job as that of
inspiring confidence, dispelling doubts, and pumping up the

national spirit of self-congratulation. If he repeatedly laid claim to a single adjective, it was "optimistic." On the occasion of his sixtieth birthday, he told reporters he was "optimistic" about a variety of foreign policy challenges, offering as an overview, "I'm optimistic that all problems will be solved." Nor did he brook any doubts or hesitations among his close advisers. According to Bob Woodward, Condoleezza Rice failed to express some of her worries because, she said, "the president almost demanded optimism. He didn't like pessimism, hand-wringing or doubt."[6]

Then things began to go wrong, which is not in itself unusual but was a possibility excluded by America's official belief that things are good and getting better. There was the dot-com bust that began a few months after Clinton's declaration of unprecedented prosperity in his final State of the Union address, then the terrorist attack of September 11, 2001. Furthermore, things began to go wrong in a way that suggested that positive thinking might not guarantee success after all, that it might in fact dim our ability to fend off real threats. In her remarkable book, *Never Saw It Coming: Cultural Challenges to Envisioning the Worst,* sociologist Karen Cerulo recounts a number of ways that the habit of positive thinking, or what she calls optimistic bias, undermined preparedness and invited disaster. She quotes *Newsweek* reporters Michael Hirsch and Michael Isikoff, for example, in their conclusion that "a whole summer of missed clues, taken together, seemed to presage the terrible September of 2001."[7] There had already been a terrorist attack on the World Trade Center in 1993; there were ample warnings, in the summer of 2001, about a possible attack by airplane, and flight schools reported suspicious students like the one who wanted to learn how to "fly a plane but didn't care about landing and takeoff." The fact that no one—the FBI, the INS, Bush, or Rice—heeded these disturbing cues was later attributed to a "failure of imagination." But actually there was plenty of imagination at work—imagining an invulnerable nation and an ever-booming economy—there was simply no ability or inclination to imagine the worst.

A similar reckless optimism pervaded the American invasion of Iraq. Warnings about possible Iraqi resistance were swept aside by leaders who promised a "cakewalk" and envisioned cheering locals greeting our troops with flowers. Likewise, Hurricane Katrina was not exactly an unanticipated disaster. In 2002, the New Orleans *Times-Picayune* ran a Pulitzer Prize–winning series warning that the city's levees could not protect it against the storm surge brought on by a category 4 or 5 hurricane. In 2001, *Scientific American* had issued a similar warning about the city's vulnerability.[8] Even when the hurricane struck and levees broke, no alarm bells went off in Washington, and when a New Orleans FEMA official sent a panicky e-mail to FEMA director Michael Brown, alerting him to the rising number of deaths and a shortage of food in the drowning city, he was told that Brown would need an hour to eat his dinner in a Baton Rouge restaurant.[9] Criminal negligence or another "failure of imagination"? The truth is that Americans had been working hard for decades to school themselves in the techniques of positive thinking, and these included the reflexive capacity for dismissing disturbing news.

The biggest "come-uppance," to use Krugman's term, has so far been the financial meltdown of 2007 and the ensuing economic crisis. By the late first decade of the twenty-first century, as we shall see in the chapters that follow, positive thinking had become ubiquitous and virtually unchallenged in American culture. It was promoted on some of the most widely watched talk shows, like *Larry King Live* and the *Oprah Winfrey Show*; it was the stuff of runaway best sellers like the 2006 book *The Secret*; it had been adopted as the theology of America's most successful evangelical preachers; it found a place in medicine as a potential adjuvant to the treatment of almost any disease. It had even penetrated the academy in the form of the new discipline of "positive psychology," offering courses teaching students to pump up their optimism and nurture their positive feelings. And its reach was growing global, first in the Anglophone countries and soon in the rising economies of China, South Korea, and India.

But nowhere did it find a warmer welcome than in American business, which is, of course, also global business. To the extent that positive thinking had become a business itself, business was its principal client, eagerly consuming the good news that all things are possible through an effort of mind. This was a useful message for employees, who by the turn of the twenty-first century were being required to work longer hours for fewer benefits and diminishing job security. But it was also a liberating ideology for top-level executives. What was the point in agonizing over balance sheets and tedious analyses of risks—and why bother worrying about dizzying levels of debt and exposure to potential defaults—when all good things come to those who are optimistic enough to expect them?

I do not write this in a spirit of sourness or personal disappointment of any kind, nor do I have any romantic attachment to suffering as a source of insight or virtue. On the contrary, I would like to see more smiles, more laughter, more hugs, more happiness and, better yet, joy. In my own vision of utopia, there is not only more comfort, and security for everyone—better jobs, health care, and so forth—there are also more parties, festivities, and opportunities for dancing in the streets. Once our basic material needs are met—in my utopia, anyway—life becomes a perpetual celebration in which everyone has a talent to contribute. But we cannot levitate ourselves into that blessed condition by wishing it. We need to brace ourselves for a struggle against terrifying obstacles, both of our own making and imposed by the natural world. And the first step is to recover from the mass delusion that is positive thinking.

ONE

Smile or Die:
The Bright Side of Cancer

The first attempt to recruit me into positive thinking occurred at what has been, so far, the low point of my life. If you had asked me, just before the diagnosis of cancer, whether I was an optimist or a pessimist, I would have been hard-pressed to answer. But on health-related matters, as it turned out, I was optimistic to the point of delusion. Nothing had so far come along that could not be controlled by diet, stretching, Advil, or, at worst, a prescription. So I was not at all alarmed when a mammogram—undertaken as part of the routine cancer surveillance all good citizens of HMOs or health plans are expected to submit to once they reach the age of fifty—aroused some "concern" on the part of the gynecologist. How could I have breast cancer? I had no known risk factors, there was no breast cancer in the family, I'd had my babies relatively young and nursed them both. I ate right, drank sparingly, worked out, and, besides, my breasts were so small that I figured a lump or two would probably improve my figure. When the gynecologist suggested a follow-up mammogram four months later, I agreed only to placate her.

I thought of it as one of those drive-by mammograms, one stop in a series of mundane missions including post office, supermarket, and gym, but I began to lose my nerve in the changing room, and not only because of the kinky necessity of baring my breasts and affixing tiny X-ray opaque stars to the tip of each nipple. The changing room, really just a closet off the stark, windowless space that housed the mammogram machine, contained something far worse, I noticed for the first time—an assumption about who I am, where I am going, and what I will need when I get there. Almost all of the eye-level space had been filled with photocopied bits of cuteness and sentimentality: pink ribbons, a cartoon about a woman with iatrogenically flattened breasts, an "Ode to a Mammogram," a list of the "Top Ten Things Only Women Understand" ("Fat Clothes" and "Eyelash Curlers," among them), and, inescapably, right next to the door, the poem "I Said a Prayer for You Today," illustrated with pink roses.

It went on and on, this mother of all mammograms, cutting into gym time, dinnertime, and lifetime generally. Sometimes the machine didn't work, and I got squished into position to no purpose at all. More often, the X-ray was successful but apparently alarming to the invisible radiologist, off in some remote office, who called the shots and never had the courtesy to show her face with an apology or an explanation. I tried pleading with the technician to speed up the process, but she just got this tight little professional smile on her face, either out of guilt for the torture she was inflicting or because she already knew something that I was going to be sorry to find out for myself. For an hour and a half the procedure was repeated: the squishing, the snapshot, the technician bustling off to consult the radiologist and returning with a demand for new angles and more definitive images. In the intervals while she was off with the doctor I read the *New York Times* right down to the personally irrelevant sections like theater and real estate, eschewing the stack of women's magazines provided for me, much as I ordinarily enjoy a quick read about sweatproof eyeliners and "fabulous sex tonight," because I had picked up this warning vibe in the changing room, which, in my increasingly anxious state, translated into: femininity is death. Finally there was nothing left to read but one of the free local weekly newspapers, where I found, buried deep in the classifieds, something even more unsettling than the growing prospect of major disease—a classified ad for a "breast cancer teddy bear" with a pink ribbon stitched to its chest.

Yes, atheists pray in their foxholes—in this case, with a yearning new to me and sharp as lust, for a clean and honorable death by shark bite, lightning strike, sniper fire, car crash. Let me be hacked to death by a madman, was my silent supplication—anything but suffocation by the pink sticky sentiment embodied in that bear and oozing from the walls of the changing room. I didn't mind dying, but the idea that I should do so while clutching a teddy and with a sweet little smile on my face—well, no amount of philosophy had prepared me for that.

The result of the mammogram, conveyed to me by phone a day later, was that I would need a biopsy, and, for some reason, a messy, surgical one with total anesthesia. Still, I was not overly perturbed and faced the biopsy like a falsely accused witch confronting a trial by dunking: at least I would clear my name. I called my children to inform them of the upcoming surgery and assured them that the great majority of lumps detected by mammogram—80 percent, the radiology technician had told me—are benign. If anything was sick, it was that creaky old mammogram machine.

My official induction into breast cancer came about ten days later with the biopsy, from which I awoke to find the surgeon standing perpendicular to me, at the far end of the gurney, down near my feet, stating gravely, "Unfortunately, there is a cancer." It took me all the rest of that drug-addled day to decide that the most heinous thing about that sentence was not the presence of cancer but the absence of me—for I, Barbara, did not enter into it even as a location, a geographical reference point. Where I once was—not a commanding presence perhaps but nonetheless a standard assemblage of flesh and words and gesture—"there is a cancer." I had been replaced by it, was the surgeon's implication. This was what I was now, medically speaking.

In my last act of dignified self-assertion, I requested to see the pathology slides myself. This was not difficult to arrange in our small-town hospital, where the pathologist turned out to be a friend of a friend, and my rusty Ph.D. in cell biology (Rockefeller University, 1968) probably helped. He was a jolly fellow, the pathologist, who called me "hon" and sat me down at one end of the dual-head microscope while he manned the other and moved a pointer through the field. These are the cancer cells, he said, showing up blue because of their overactive DNA. Most of them were arranged in staid semicircular arrays, like suburban houses squeezed into cul-de-sacs, but I also saw what I knew enough to know I did not want to see: the characteristic "Indian files" of cells on the march. The "enemy," I was supposed to think—an image to save up for future exercises in "visualization" of their violent deaths at the hands of the body's killer cells, the lymphocytes and macrophages.

But I was impressed, against all rational self-interest, by the energy of these cellular conga lines, their determination to move on out from the backwater of the breast to colonize lymph nodes, bone marrow, lungs, and brain. These are, after all, the fanatics of Barbara-ness, the rebel cells that have realized that the genome they carry, the genetic essence of me in whatever deranged form,

has no further chance of normal reproduction in the postmenopausal body we share, so why not just start multiplying like bun-
nies and hope for a chance to break out?

After the visit to the pathologist, my biological curiosity dropped
to a lifetime nadir. I know women who followed up their diagnoses with weeks or months of self-study, mastering their options,
interviewing doctor after doctor, assessing the damage to be expected from the available treatments. But I could tell from a few
hours of investigation that the career of a breast cancer patient
had been pretty well mapped out in advance: you may get to nego-
tiate the choice between lumpectomy and mastectomy, but lumpectomy is commonly followed by weeks of radiation, and in either
case if the lymph nodes turn out, upon dissection, to be invaded—
or "involved," as it's less threateningly put—you're doomed to
months of chemotherapy, an intervention that is on a par with using a sledge hammer to swat mosquitoes. Chemotherapy agents
damage and kill not just cancer cells but any normal body cells
that happen to be dividing, such as those in the skin, hair follicles,
stomach lining, and bone marrow (which is the source of all blood
cells, including immune cells). The results are baldness, nausea,
mouth sores, immunosuppression, and, in many cases, anemia.

These interventions do not constitute a "cure" or anything
close, which is why the death rate from breast cancer had changed
very little between the 1930s, when mastectomy was the only treatment available, and 2000, when I received my diagnosis. Chemotherapy, which became a routine part of breast cancer treatment
in the eighties, does not confer anywhere near as decisive an advantage as patients are often led to believe. It's most helpful for
younger, premenopausal women, who can gain a 7 to 11 percentage point increase in ten-year survival rates, but most breast cancer victims are older, postmenopausal women like myself, for
whom chemotherapy adds only a 2 or 3 percentage point difference,

according to America's best-known breast cancer surgeon, Susan Love.[1] So yes, it might add a few months to your life, but it also condemns you to many months of low-level sickness.

In fact, there's been a history of struggle over breast cancer treatments. In the seventies, doctors were still performing radical mastectomies that left patients permanently disabled on the affected side—until women's health activists protested, insisting on less radical, "modified" mastectomies. It had also been the practice to go directly from biopsy to mastectomy while the patient was anesthetized and unable to make any decisions—again, until enough women protested. Then, in the nineties, there was a brief fad of treating patients whose cancers had metastasized by destroying all their bone marrow with high-dose chemotherapy and replacing it with bone marrow transplants—an intervention that largely served to hasten the patient's death. Chemotherapy, radiation, and so on may represent state-of-the-art care today, but so, at one point in medical history, did the application of leeches.

I knew these bleak facts, or sort of knew them, but in the fog of anesthesia that hung over those first few weeks, I seemed to lose my capacity for self-defense. The pressure was on, from doctors and loved ones, to do something right away—kill it, get it out now. The endless exams, the bone scan to check for metastases, the high-tech heart test to see if I was strong enough to withstand chemotherapy—all these blurred the line between selfhood and thing-hood anyway, organic and inorganic, me and it. As my cancer career unfolded, I would, the helpful pamphlets explain, become a composite of the living and the dead—an implant to replace the breast, a wig to replace the hair. And then what will I mean when I use the word "I"? I fell into a state of unreasoning passive aggressivity: They diagnosed this, so it's their baby. They found it, let them fix it.

I could take my chances with "alternative" treatments, of course, like punk novelist Kathy Acker, who succumbed to breast cancer in 1997 after a course of alternative therapies in Mexico, or actress and ThighMaster promoter Suzanne Somers, who made tabloid headlines by injecting herself with mistletoe brew. But I have never admired the "natural" or believed in the "wisdom of the body." Death is as "natural" as anything gets, and the body has always seemed to me like a retarded Siamese twin dragging along behind me, a hysteric really, dangerously overreacting, in my case, to everyday allergens and minute ingestions of sugar. I would put my faith in science, even if this meant that the dumb old body was about to be transmogrified into an evil clown—puking, trembling, swelling, surrendering significant parts, and oozing postsurgical fluids. The surgeon—a more genial and forthcoming one this time—could fit me in; the oncologist would see me. Welcome to Cancerland.

The Pink Ribbon Culture

Fortunately, no one has to go through this alone. Forty years ago, before Betty Ford, Rose Kushner, Betty Rollin, and other pioneer patients spoke out, breast cancer was a dread secret, endured in silence and euphemized in obituaries as a "long illness." Something about the conjuncture of "breast," signifying sexuality and nurturance, and that other word, suggesting the claws of a devouring crustacean, spooked almost everyone. Today, however, it's the biggest disease on the cultural map, bigger than AIDS, cystic fibrosis, or spinal injury, bigger even than those more prolific killers of women—heart disease, lung cancer, and stroke. There are roughly hundreds of Web sites devoted to it, not to mention newsletters, support groups, a whole genre of first-person breast cancer books, even a glossy upper-middle-brow monthly magazine, *Mamm*. There are four major national breast cancer organizations, of which the mightiest, in financial terms, is the Susan G. Komen Foundation, headed by breast cancer survivor and Republican donor Nancy Brinker. Komen organizes the annual Race for the Cure®, which attracts about a million people—mostly survivors, friends, and family members. Its Web site provides a microcosm of the breast cancer culture, offering news of the races, message boards for accounts of individuals' struggles with the disease, and uplifting inspirational messages.

The first thing I discovered as I waded out into the relevant sites is that not everyone views the disease with horror and dread. Instead, the appropriate attitude is upbeat and even eagerly acquisitive. There are between two and three million American women in various stages of breast cancer treatment, who, along with anxious relatives, make up a significant market for all things breast cancer related. Bears, for example: I identified four distinct lines, or species, of these creatures, including Carol, the Remembrance Bear; Hope, the Breast Cancer Research Bear, which wore a pink turban as if to conceal chemotherapy-induced baldness; the Susan Bear, named for Nancy Brinker's deceased sister; and the Nick and Nora Wish Upon a Star Bear, which was available, along with the Susan Bear, at the Komen Foundation Web site's "marketplace."

And bears are only the tip, so to speak, of the cornucopia of pink-ribbon-themed breast cancer products. You can dress in pink-beribboned sweatshirts, denim shirts, pajamas, lingerie, aprons, loungewear, shoelaces, and socks; accessorize with pink rhinestone brooches, angel pins, scarves, caps, earrings, and bracelets; brighten up your home with breast cancer candles, stained glass pink-ribbon candleholders, coffee mugs, pendants, wind chimes, and night-lights; and pay your bills with Checks for the Cure™. "Awareness" beats secrecy and stigma, of course, but I couldn't help noticing that the existential space in which a friend had earnestly advised me to "confront [my] mortality" bore a striking resemblance to the mall.

This is not entirely, I should point out, a case of cynical merchants exploiting the sick. Some of the breast cancer tchotchkes and accessories are made by breast cancer survivors themselves, such as "Janice," creator of the Daisy Awareness Necklace, among other things, and in most cases a portion of the sales goes to breast cancer research. Virginia Davis of Aurora, Colorado, was inspired to create the Remembrance Bear by a friend's double mastectomy and told me she sees her work as more of a "crusade" than a business. When I interviewed her in 2001, she was expecting to ship ten thousand of these teddies, which are manufactured in China, and send part of the money to the Race for the Cure. If the bears are infantilizing—as I tried ever so tactfully to suggest was how they may, in rare cases, be perceived—so far no one had complained. "I just get love letters," she told me, "from people who say, 'God bless you for thinking of us.'"

The ultrafeminine theme of the breast cancer marketplace—the prominence, for example, of cosmetics and jewelry—could be understood as a response to the treatments' disastrous effects on one's looks. No doubt, too, all the prettiness and pinkness is meant to inspire a positive outlook. But the infantilizing trope is a little harder to account for, and teddy bears are not its only manifestation. A tote bag distributed to breast cancer patients by the Libby Ross Foundation (through places such as the Columbia-Presbyterian Medical Center) contained, among other items, a tube of Estée Lauder Perfumed Body Crème, a hot pink satin pillowcase, a small tin of peppermint pastilles, a set of three small, inexpensive rhinestone bracelets, a pink-striped "journal and sketch book," and—somewhat jarringly—a box of crayons. Marla Willner, one of the founders of the Libby Ross Foundation, told me that the crayons "go with the journal—for people to express different moods, different thoughts," though she admitted she has never tried to write with crayons herself. Possibly the idea was that regression to a state of childlike dependency puts one in the best frame of mind for enduring the prolonged and toxic treatments. Or it may be that, in some versions of the prevailing gender ideology, femininity is by its nature incompatible with full adulthood—a state of arrested development. Certainly men diagnosed with prostate cancer do not receive gifts of Matchbox cars.

But I, no less than the bear huggers, needed whatever help I could get and found myself searching obsessively for practical tips on hair loss, how to select a chemotherapy regimen, what to wear after surgery and eat when the scent of food sucks. There was, I soon discovered, far more than I could usefully absorb, for thousands of the afflicted have posted their stories, beginning with the lump or bad mammogram, proceeding through the agony of the treatments, pausing to mention the sustaining forces of family, humor, and religion, and ending, in almost all cases, with an upbeat message for the terrified neophyte. Some of these are no more than a paragraph long—brief waves from sister sufferers. Others offer almost hour-by-hour logs of breast-deprived, chemotherapized lives:

> Tuesday, August 15, 2000: Well, I survived my 4th chemo. Very, very dizzy today. Very nauseated, but no barfing! It's a first. . . . I break out in a cold sweat and my heart pounds if I stay up longer than 5 minutes.

> Friday, August 18, 2000: . . . By dinnertime, I was full out nauseated. I took some meds and ate a rice and vegetable bowl from Trader Joe's. It smelled and tasted

awful to me, but I ate it anyway. . . . Rick brought home
some Kern's nectars and I'm drinking that. Seems to
have settled my stomach a little bit.

I couldn't seem to get enough of these tales, reading on with
panicky fascination about everything that can go wrong—
septicemia, ruptured implants, startling recurrences a few years
after the completion of treatments, "mets" (metastases) to vital
organs, and—what scared me most in the short term—"chemo
brain," or the cognitive deterioration that sometimes accompa-
nies chemotherapy. I compared myself with everyone, selfishly
impatient with those whose conditions were less menacing, shiv-
ering over those who had reached Stage IV ("There is no Stage V,"
as the main character in the play *Wit*, who has ovarian cancer,
explains), constantly assessing my chances.

But, despite all the helpful information, the more fellow victims I discovered and read, the greater my sense of isolation grew.
No one among the bloggers and book writers seemed to share my
sense of outrage over the disease and the available treatments.
What causes it and why is it so common, especially in industrialized societies?* Why don't we have treatments that distinguish
between different forms of breast cancer or between cancer cells

---

* "Bad" genes of the inherited variety are thought to account for less than 10 percent of
breast cancers, and only 30 percent of women diagnosed with breast cancer have any
known risk factor (such as delaying childbearing or the late onset of menopause) at all. Bad
lifestyle choices like a fatty diet have, after brief popularity with the medical profession,
been largely ruled out. Hence, groups like Breast Cancer Action argue, suspicion should
focus on environmental carcinogens, such as plastics, pesticides (DDT and PCBs, for example, though banned in this country, are still used in many Third World sources of the
produce we eat), and the industrial runoff in our ground water. No carcinogen has been
linked definitely to human breast cancer yet, but many carcinogens have been found to
cause the disease in mice, and the inexorable increase of the disease in industrialized
nations—about 1 percent a year between the 1950s and the 1990s—further hints at environmental factors, as does the fact that women migrants to industrialized countries
quickly develop the same breast cancer rates as those who are native-born.

and normal dividing cells? In the mainstream of breast cancer culture, there is very little anger, no mention of possible environmental causes, and few comments about the fact that, in all but the more advanced, metastasized cases, it is the "treatments," not the disease, that cause the immediate illness and pain. In fact, the overall tone is almost universally upbeat. The Breast Friends Web site, for example, featured a series of inspirational quotes: "Don't cry over anything that can't cry over you," "I can't stop the birds of sorrow from circling my head, but I can stop them from building a nest in my hair," "When life hands out lemons, squeeze out a smile," "Don't wait for your ship to come in . . . swim out to meet it," and much more of that ilk. Even in the relatively sophisticated *Mamm*, a columnist bemoaned not cancer or chemotherapy but the end of chemotherapy and humorously proposed to deal with her separation anxiety by pitching a tent outside her oncologist's office. Positive thinking seems to be mandatory in the breast cancer world, to the point that unhappiness requires a kind of apology, as when "Lucy," whose "long-term prognosis is not good," started her personal narrative on breastcancertalk.org by telling us that her story "is not the usual one, full of sweetness and hope, but true nevertheless."

Even the word "victim" is proscribed, leaving no single noun to describe a woman with breast cancer. As in the AIDS movement, upon which breast cancer activism is partly modeled, the words "patient" and "victim," with their aura of self-pity and passivity, have been ruled un-P.C. Instead, we get verbs: those who are in the midst of their treatments are described as "battling" or "fighting," sometimes intensified with "bravely" or "fiercely"—language suggestive of Katharine Hepburn with her face to the wind. Once the treatments are over, one achieves the status of "survivor," which is how the women in my local support group identified themselves, A.A.-style, when we convened to share war stories and rejoice in our "survivorhood": "Hi, I'm Kathy and I'm a three-year survivor." My support group seemed supportive enough, but some women have reported being expelled by their groups when their cancers metastasized and it became clear they would never graduate to the rank of "survivor."[2]

For those who cease to be survivors and join the more than forty thousand American women who succumb to breast cancer each year—again, no noun applies. They are said to have "lost their battle" and may be memorialized by photographs carried at races for the cure—our lost brave sisters, our fallen soldiers. But in the overwhelmingly positive culture that has grown up around breast cancer, martyrs count for little; it is the "survivors" who merit constant honor and acclaim. At a "Relay for Life" event in my town, sponsored by the American Cancer Society, the dead were present only in much diminished form. A series of paper bags, each about the right size for a junior burger and fries, lined the relay track. On them were the names of the dead, and inside each was a candle that was lit after dark, when the actual relay race began. The stars, though, were the runners, the "survivors," who seemed to offer living proof the disease isn't so bad after all.

Embracing Cancer

The cheerfulness of breast cancer culture goes beyond mere absence of anger to what looks, all too often, like a positive embrace of the disease. As "Mary" reports, on the Bosom Buds message board: "I really believe I am a much more sensitive and thoughtful person now. It might sound funny but I was a real worrier before. Now I don't want to waste my energy on worrying. I enjoy life so much more now and in a lot of aspects I am much happier now." Or this from "Andee": "This was the hardest year of my life but also in many ways the most rewarding. I got rid of the baggage, made peace with my family, met many amazing people, learned to take very good care of my body so it will take care of me, and reprioritized my life." Cindy Cherry, quoted in the *Washington Post*, goes further: "If I had to do it over, would I want breast cancer? Absolutely. I'm not the same person I was, and I'm glad I'm not. Money doesn't matter anymore. I've met the most phenomenal people in my life through this. Your friends and family are what matter now."[3]

The First Year of the Rest of Your Life, a collection of brief narratives with a foreword by Nancy Brinker and a share of the royalties going to the Komen Foundation, is filled with such testimonies to the redemptive powers of the disease: "I can honestly say I am happier now than I have ever been in my life—even before the breast cancer"; "For me, breast cancer has provided a good kick in the rear to get me started rethinking my life"; "I have come out stronger, with a new sense of priorities."[4] Never a complaint about lost time, shattered sexual confidence, or the long-term weakening of the arms caused by lymph node dissection and radiation. What does not destroy you, to paraphrase Nietzsche, makes you a spunkier, more evolved sort of person.

Writing in 2007, *New York Times* health columnist Jane Brody faithfully reflected the near universal bright-siding of the disease.[5] She gave a nod to the downside of breast cancer and cancer generally: "It can cause considerable physical and emotional pain and lasting disfigurement. It may even end in death." But for the most part her column was a veritable ode to the uplifting effects of cancer, and especially breast cancer. She quoted bike racer and testicular cancer survivor Lance Armstrong saying, "Cancer was the best thing that ever happened to me," and cited a woman asserting that "breast cancer has given me a new life. Breast cancer was something I needed to experience to open my eyes to the joy of living. I now see more of the world than I was choosing to see before I had cancer. . . . Breast cancer has taught me to love in the purest sense." Betty Rollin, one of the first women to go public with her disease, was enlisted to testify that she has "realized that the source of my happiness was, of all things, cancer—that cancer had everything to do with how good the good parts of my life were."

In the most extreme characterization, breast cancer is not a problem at all, not even an annoyance—it is a "gift," deserving of the most heartfelt gratitude. One survivor turned author credits it with revelatory powers, writing in her book *The Gift of Cancer: A Call to Awakening* that "cancer is your ticket to your real life. Cancer is your passport to the life you were truly meant to live." And if that is not enough to make you want to go out and get an injection of live cancer cells, she insists, "Cancer will lead you to God. Let me say that again. Cancer is your connection to the Divine."[6]

The effect of all this positive thinking is to transform breast cancer into a rite of passage—not an injustice or a tragedy to rail against but a normal marker in the life cycle, like menopause or grandmotherhood. Everything in mainstream breast cancer culture serves, no doubt inadvertently, to tame and normalize the disease: the diagnosis may be disastrous, but there are those cunning pink rhinestone angel pins to buy and races to train for. Even the heavy traffic in personal narratives and practical tips that I found so useful bears an implicit acceptance of the disease and the current clumsy and barbarous approaches to its treatment: you can get so busy comparing attractive head scarves that you forget to question whether chemotherapy is really going to be effective in your case. Understood as a rite of passage, breast cancer resembles the initiation rites so exhaustively studied by Mircea Eliade. First there is the selection of the initiates—by age in the tribal situation, by mammogram or palpation here. Then come

the requisite ordeals—scarification or circumcision within traditional cultures, surgery and chemotherapy for the cancer patient.
Finally, the initiate emerges into a new and higher status—an adult
and a warrior—or in the case of breast cancer, a "survivor."

And in our implacably optimistic breast cancer culture, the disease offers more than the intangible benefits of spiritual upward
mobility. You can defy the inevitable disfigurements and come
out, on the survivor side, actually prettier, sexier, more femme. In
the lore of the disease—shared with me by oncology nurses as
well as by survivors—chemotherapy smoothes and tightens the
skin and helps you lose weight, and, when your hair comes back
it will be fuller, softer, easier to control, and perhaps a surprising
new color. These may be myths, but for those willing to get with the
prevailing program, opportunities for self-improvement abound.
The American Cancer Society offers the "Look Good . . . Feel Better" program, "dedicated to teaching women cancer patients beauty
techniques to help restore their appearance and self-image during cancer treatment." Thirty thousand women participate a year,
each copping a free makeover and bag of makeup donated by the
Cosmetic, Toiletry, and Fragrance Association, the trade association of the cosmetics industry. As for that lost breast: after reconstruction, why not bring the other one up to speed? Of the more
than fifty thousand mastectomy patients who opt for reconstruction each year, 17 percent go on, often at the urging of their plastic
surgeons, to get additional surgery so that the remaining breast
will "match" the more erect and perhaps larger new structure on
the other side.

Not everyone goes for cosmetic deceptions, and the question
of wigs versus baldness, reconstruction versus undisguised scar,
defines one of the few real disagreements in breast cancer culture. On the more avant-garde, upper-middle-class side, *Mamm*

magazine—in which literary critic Eve Kosofsky Sedgwick served as a columnist—tends to favor the "natural" look. Here, mastectomy scars can be "sexy" and baldness something to celebrate. A cover story featured women who "looked upon their baldness not just as a loss, but also as an opportunity: to indulge their playful sides . . . to come in contact, in new ways, with their truest selves." One woman decorated her scalp with temporary tattoos of peace signs, panthers, and frogs; another expressed herself with a shocking purple wig; a third reported that unadorned baldness made her feel "sensual, powerful, able to recreate myself with every new day." But no hard feelings toward those who choose to hide their condition under wigs or scarves; it's just a matter, *Mamm* tells us, of "different aesthetics." Some go for pink ribbons; others will prefer the Ralph Lauren Pink Pony breast cancer motif. But everyone agrees that breast cancer is a chance for creative self-transformation—a makeover opportunity, in fact.

In the seamless world of breast cancer culture, where one Web site links to another—from personal narratives and grassroots endeavors to the glitzy level of corporate sponsors and celebrity spokespeople—cheerfulness is required, dissent a kind of treason. Within this tightly knit world, attitudes are subtly adjusted, doubters gently brought back to the fold. In *The First Year of the Rest of Your Life*, for example, each personal narrative is followed by a study question or tip designed to counter the slightest hint of negativity—and they are very slight hints indeed, since the collection includes no harridans, whiners, or feminist militants:

> Have you given yourself permission to acknowledge
> you have some anxiety or "blues" and to ask for help
> for your emotional well-being? . . .

> Is there an area in your life of unresolved internal
> conflict? Is there an area where you think you might
> want to do some "healthy mourning"? . . .
>
> Try keeping a list of the things you find "good about
> today."[7]

As an experiment, I posted a statement on the Komen.org
message board, under the subject line "Angry," briefly listing my
complaints about the debilitating effects of chemotherapy, recalcitrant insurance companies, environmental carcinogens, and,
most daringly, "sappy pink ribbons." I received a few words of
encouragement in my fight with the insurance company, which
had taken the position that my biopsy was a kind of optional in-
dulgence, but mostly a chorus of rebukes. "Suzy" wrote to tell me,
"I really dislike saying you have a bad attitude towards all of this,
but you do, and it's not going to help you in the least." "Mary" was
a bit more tolerant, writing, "Barb, at this time in your life, it's so
important to put all your energies toward a peaceful, if not happy,
existence. Cancer is a rotten thing to have happen and there are
no answers for any of us as to why. But to live your life, whether
you have one more year or 51, in anger and bitterness is such a
waste. . . . I hope you can find some peace. You deserve it. We all
do. God bless you and keep you in His loving care. Your sister,
Mary."

"Kitty," however, thought I'd gone around the bend: "You need
to run, not walk, to some counseling. . . . Please, get yourself some
help and I ask everyone on this site to pray for you so you can enjoy life to the fullest." The only person who offered me any reinforcement was "Gerri," who had been through all the treatments
and now found herself in terminal condition, with only a few
months of life remaining: "I am also angry. All the money that is
raised, all the smiling faces of survivors who make it sound like it

is o.k. to have breast cancer. IT IS NOT O.K.!" But Gerri's message, like the others on the message board, was posted under the inadvertently mocking heading "What does it mean to be a breast cancer survivor?"

The "Scientific" Argument for Cheer

There was, I learned, an urgent medical reason to embrace cancer with a smile: a "positive attitude" is supposedly essential to recovery. During the months when I was undergoing chemotherapy, I encountered this assertion over and over—on Web sites, in books, from oncology nurses and fellow sufferers. Eight years later, it remains almost axiomatic, within the breast cancer culture, that survival hinges on "attitude." One study found 60 percent of women who had been treated for the disease attributing their continued survival to a "positive attitude."[8] In articles and on their Web sites, individuals routinely take pride in this supposedly lifesaving mental state. "The key is all about having a positive attitude, which I've tried to have since the beginning," a woman named Sherry Young says in an article entitled "Positive Attitude Helped Woman Beat Cancer."[9]

"Experts" of various sorts offer a plausible-sounding explanation for the salubrious properties of cheerfulness. A recent e-zine article entitled "Breast Cancer Prevention Tips"—and the notion of breast cancer "prevention" should itself set off alarms, since there is no known means of prevention—for example, advises that:

> A simple positive and optimistic attitude has been shown to reduce the risk of cancer. This will sound amazing to many people; however, it will suffice to explain that several medical studies have demonstrated the link between a positive attitude and an

improved immune system. Laughter and humor has
[*sic*] been shown to enhance the body's immunity
and prevents against cancer and other diseases. You
must have heard the slogan "happy people don't fall
sick."[10]

No wonder my "angry" post was greeted with so much dismay on
the Komen site: my respondents no doubt believed that a positive
attitude boosts the immune system, empowering it to battle cancer more effectively.

You've probably read that assertion so often, in one form or
another, that it glides by without a moment's thought about what
the immune system is, how it might be affected by emotions, and
what, if anything, it could do to fight cancer. The business of the
immune system is to defend the body against foreign intruders,
such as microbes, and it does so with a huge onslaught of cells
and whole cascades of different molecular weapons. The complexity, and diversity, of the mobilization is overwhelming: Whole
tribes and subtribes of cells assemble at the site of infection, each
with its own form of weaponry, resembling one of the ram-
shackle armies in the movie *The Chronicles of Narnia*. Some of
these warrior cells toss a bucket of toxins at the invader and then
move on; others are there to nourish their comrades with chemical spritzers. The body's lead warriors, the macrophages, close in
on their prey, envelop it in their own "flesh," and digest it. As it
happens, macrophages were the topic of my Ph.D. thesis; they are
large, mobile, amoebalike creatures capable of living for months
or years. When the battle is over, they pass on information about
the intruder to other cells, which will produce antibodies to speed
up the body's defenses in the next encounter. They will also eat
not only the vanquished intruders but their own dead comrades-
in-arms.

For all its dizzying complexity—which has kept other graduate students toiling away "at the bench" for decades—the immune system is hardly foolproof. Some invaders, like the tuberculosis bacillus, outwit it by penetrating the body's tissue cells and setting up shop inside them, where the bacilli cannot be detected by immune cells. Most diabolically, the HIV virus selectively attacks certain immune cells, rendering the body almost defenseless. And sometimes the immune system perversely turns against the body's own tissues, causing such "autoimmune" diseases as lupus and rheumatoid arthritis and possibly some forms of heart disease. It may not be perfect, this seemingly anarchic system of cellular defense, but it is what has evolved so far out of a multimillion-year arms race with our microbial enemies.

The link between the immune system, cancer, and the emotions was cobbled together somewhat imaginatively in the 1970s. It had been known for some time that extreme stress could debilitate certain aspects of the immune system. Torture a lab animal long enough, as the famous stress investigator Hans Selye did in the 1930s, and it becomes less healthy and resistant to disease. It was apparently a short leap, for many, to the conclusion that positive feelings might be the opposite of stress—capable of boosting the immune system and providing the key to health, whether the threat is a microbe or a tumor.

One of the early best-selling assertions of this notion was *Getting Well Again,* by O. Carl Simonton, an oncologist; Stephanie Matthews-Simonton, identified in the book as a "motivational counselor"; and psychologist James L. Creighton. So confident were they of the immune system's ability to defeat cancer that they believed "a cancer does not require just the presence of abnormal cells, it also requires a *suppression of the body's normal defenses.*"[11] What could suppress them? Stress. While the Simontons urged cancer patients to obediently comply with the prescribed treatments, they

suggested that a kind of attitude adjustment was equally important. Stress had to be overcome, positive beliefs and mental imag-
ery acquired.

The Simontons' book was followed in 1986 by surgeon Bernie
Siegel's even more exuberant *Love, Medicine, and Miracles*, offering
the view that "a vigorous immune system can overcome cancer
if it is not interfered with, and emotional growth toward greater
self-acceptance and fulfillment helps keep the immune system
strong."[12] Hence cancer was indeed a blessing, since it could force
the victim into adopting a more positive and loving view of the
world.

But where were the studies showing the healing effect of a
positive attitude? Could they be duplicated? One of the skeptics,
Stanford psychiatrist David Spiegel, told me he set out in 1989 to
refute the popular dogma that attitude could overcome cancer. "I
was so sick of hearing Bernie Siegel saying that you got cancer
because you needed it," he told me in an interview. But to his surprise, Spiegel's study showed that breast cancer patients in support groups—who presumably were in a better frame of mind than
those facing the disease on their own—lived longer than those in
the control group. Spiegel promptly interrupted the study, decid-
ing that no one should be deprived of the benefits provided by a
support group. The dogma was affirmed and remained so at the
time I was diagnosed.

You can see its appeal. First, the idea of a link between subjective feelings and the disease gave the breast cancer patient something to *do*. Instead of waiting passively for the treatments to kick
in, she had her own work to do—on herself. She had to monitor
her moods and mobilize psychic energy for the war at the cellular
level. In the Simontons' scheme, she was to devote part of each day
to drawing cartoonish sketches of battles among buglike cells. If
the cancer cells were not depicted as "very weak [and] confused"

and the body's immune cells were not portrayed as "strong and aggressive," the patient could be courting death, and had more work to do.[13] At the same time, the dogma created expanded opportunities in the cancer research and treatment industry: not only surgeons and oncologists were needed but behavioral scientists, therapists, motivational counselors, and people willing to write exhortatory self-help books.

The dogma, however, did not survive further research. In the nineties, studies began to roll in refuting Spiegel's 1989 work on the curative value of support groups. The amazing survival rates of women in Spiegel's first study turned out to be a fluke. Then, in the May 2007 issue of *Psychological Bulletin*, James Coyne and two coauthors published the results of a systematic review of all the literature on the supposed effects of psychotherapy on cancer. The idea was that psychotherapy, like a support group, should help the patient improve her mood and decrease her level of stress. But Coyne and his coauthors found the existing literature full of "endemic problems."[14] In fact, there seemed to be no positive effect of therapy at all. A few months later, a team led by David Spiegel himself reported in the journal *Cancer* that support groups conferred no survival advantage after all, effectively contradicting his earlier finding. Psychotherapy and support groups might improve one's mood, but they did nothing to overcome cancer. "If cancer patients want psychotherapy or to be in a support group, they should be given the opportunity to do so," Coyne said in a summary of his research. "There can be lots of emotional and social benefits. But they should not seek such experiences solely on the expectation that they are extending their lives."[15]

When I asked Coyne in early 2009 whether there is a continuing scientific bias in favor of a link between emotions and cancer survival, he said:

> To borrow a term used to describe the buildup to the
> Iraq war, I would say there's a kind of "incestuous am-
> plification." It's very exciting—the idea that the mind
> can affect the body—and it's a way for the behavioral
> scientists to ride the train. There's a lot at stake here in
> grants for cancer-related research, and the behavioral
> scientists are clinging to it. What else do they have to
> contribute [to the fight against cancer]? Research on
> how to get people to use sunscreen? That's not sexy.

He feels that the bias is especially strong in the United States, where skeptics tend to be marginalized. "It's much easier for me to get speaking gigs in Europe," he told me.

What about the heroic battles between immune cells and cancer cells that patients are encouraged to visualize? In 1970, the famed Australian medical researcher McFarlane Burnet had proposed that the immune system is engaged in constant "surveillance" for cancer cells, which, supposedly, it would destroy upon detection. Presumably, the immune system was engaged in busily destroying cancer cells—until the day came when it was too exhausted (for example, by stress) to eliminate the renegades. There was at least one a priori problem with this hypothesis: unlike microbes, cancer cells are not "foreign"; they are ordinary tissue cells that have mutated and are not necessarily recognizable as enemy cells. As a recent editorial in the *Journal of Clinical Oncology* put it: "What we must first remember is that the immune system is designed to detect foreign invaders, and avoid our own cells. With few exceptions, the immune system does not appear to recognize cancers within an individual as foreign, because they are actually part of the self."[16]

More to the point, there is no consistent evidence that the immune system fights cancers, with the exception of those cancers caused by viruses, which may be more truly "foreign." People whose immune systems have been depleted by HIV or animals rendered immunodeficient are not especially susceptible to cancer, as the "immune surveillance" theory would predict. Nor would it make much sense to treat cancer with chemotherapy, which suppresses the immune system, if the latter were truly crucial to fighting the disease. Furthermore, no one has found a way to cure cancer by boosting the immune system with chemical or biological agents. Yes, immune cells such as macrophages can often be found clustering at tumor sites, but not always to do anything useful.

To my intense shock and dismay as a former cellular immunologist, recent research shows that macrophages may even *go over to the other side*. Instead of killing the cancer cells, they start releasing growth factors and performing other tasks that actually encourage tumor growth. Mice can be bred to be highly susceptible to breast cancer, but their incipient tumors do not become malignant without the assistance of macrophages arriving at the site.[17] A 2007 article in *Scientific American* concluded that at best "the immune system functions as a double-edged sword. . . . Sometimes it promotes cancer; other times it hinders disease."[18] Two years later, researchers discovered that another type of immune cell, lymphocytes, also promote the spread of breast cancer.[19] All those visualizations of courageous immune cells battling cancer cells missed the real drama—the seductions, the whispered deals, the betrayals.

Continuing in an anthropomorphic vein, there's an interesting parallel between macrophages and cancer cells: compared with the body's other cells, both are fiercely autonomous. Ordinary, "good" cells slavishly subject themselves to the demands of the dictatorship of the body: cardiac cells ceaselessly contract to keep the heart beating; intestinal lining cells selflessly pass on nutrients that they might have enjoyed eating themselves. But the cancer cells rip up their orders and start reproducing like independent organisms, while the macrophages are by nature free-ranging adventurers, perhaps the body's equivalent of mercenaries. If nothing else, the existence of both is a reminder that the body is in some ways more like a loose, unstable federation of cells than the disciplined, well-integrated unit of our imaginings.

And, from an evolutionary perspective, why *should* the body possess a means of combating cancer, such as a form of "natural healing" that would kick in if only we get past our fears and negative thoughts? Cancer tends to strike older people who have passed the age of reproduction and hence are of little or no evolutionary significance. Our immune system evolved to fight bacteria and viruses and does a reasonably good job of saving the young from diseases like measles, whooping cough, and the flu. If you live long enough to get cancer, chances are you will have already accomplished your biological mission and produced a few children of your own.

It could be argued that positive thinking can't hurt, that it might even be a blessing to the sorely afflicted. Who would begrudge the optimism of a dying person who clings to the hope of a last-minute remission? Or of a bald and nauseated chemotherapy patient who imagines that the cancer experience will end up giving her a more fulfilling life? Unable to actually help cure the disease, psychologists looked for ways to increase such positive feelings about cancer, which they termed "benefit finding."[20] Scales of benefit finding have been devised and dozens of articles published on the therapeutic interventions that help produce it. If you can't count on recovering, you should at least come to see your cancer as a positive experience, and this notion has been extended to other forms of cancer too. For example, prostate cancer researcher Stephen Strum has written: "You may not believe this, but prostate cancer is an opportunity. . . . [It] is a path, a model, a paradigm, of how you can interact to help yourself, and another. By doing so, you evolve to a much higher level of humanity."[21]

But rather than providing emotional sustenance, the sugar-coating of cancer can exact a dreadful cost. First, it requires the denial of understandable feelings of anger and fear, all of which must be buried under a cosmetic layer of cheer. This is a great convenience for health workers and even friends of the afflicted, who might prefer fake cheer to complaining, but it is not so easy on the afflicted. Two researchers on benefit finding report that the breast cancer patients they have worked with "have mentioned repeatedly that they view even well-intentioned efforts to encourage benefit-finding as insensitive and inept. They are almost always interpreted as an unwelcome attempt to minimize the unique burdens and challenges that need to be overcome."[22] One 2004 study even found, in complete contradiction to the tenets of positive thinking, that women who perceive more benefits from their cancer "tend to face a poorer quality of life—including worse mental functioning—compared with women who do not perceive benefits from their diagnoses."[23]

Besides, it takes effort to maintain the upbeat demeanor expected by others—effort that can no longer be justified as a contribution to long-term survival. Consider the woman who wrote to Deepak Chopra that her breast cancer had spread to the bones and lungs:

> Even though I follow the treatments, have come a long way in unburdening myself of toxic feelings, have forgiven everyone, changed my lifestyle to include

> meditation, prayer, proper diet, exercise, and supple-
> ments, the cancer keeps coming back.
>
> Am I missing a lesson here that it keeps reoccur-
> ring? I am positive I am going to beat it, yet it does get
> harder with each diagnosis to keep a positive attitude.

She was working as hard as she could—meditating, praying, forgiving—but apparently not hard enough. Chopra's response: "As far as I can tell, you are doing all the right things to recover. You just have to continue doing them until the cancer is gone for good. I know it is discouraging to make great progress only to have it come back again, but sometimes cancer is simply very pernicious and requires the utmost diligence and persistence to eventually overcome it."[24]

But others in the cancer care business have begun to speak out against what one has called "the tyranny of positive thinking." When a 2004 study found no survival benefits for optimism among lung cancer patients, its lead author, Penelope Schofield, wrote: "We should question whether it is valuable to encourage optimism if it results in the patient concealing his or her distress in the misguided belief that this will afford survival benefits. . . . If a patient feels generally pessimistic . . . it is important to acknowledge these feelings as valid and acceptable."[25]

Whether repressed feelings are themselves harmful, as many psychologists claim, I'm not so sure, but without question there is a problem when positive thinking "fails" and the cancer spreads or eludes treatment. Then the patient can only blame herself: she is not being positive enough; possibly it was her negative attitude that brought on the disease in the first place. At this point, the exhortation to think positively is "an additional burden to an already devastated patient," as oncology nurse Cynthia Rittenberg has written.[26] Jimmie Holland, a psychiatrist at Memorial Sloan-

Kettering Cancer Center in New York, writes that cancer patients experience a kind of victim blaming:

> It began to be clear to me about ten years ago that society was placing another undue and inappropriate burden on patients that seemed to come out of the popular beliefs about the mind-body connection. I would find patients coming in with stories of being told by well-meaning friends, "I've read all about this—if you got cancer, you must have wanted it. . . ." Even more distressing was the person who said, "I know I have to be positive all the time and that is the only way to cope with cancer—but it's so hard to do. I know that if I get sad, or scared or upset, I am making my tumor grow faster and I will have shortened my life."[27]

Clearly, the failure to think positively can weigh on a cancer patient like a second disease.

I, at least, was saved from this additional burden by my persistent anger—which would have been even stronger if I had suspected, as I do now, that my cancer was iatrogenic, that is, caused by the medical profession. When I was diagnosed I had been taking hormone replacement therapy for almost eight years, prescribed by doctors who avowed it would prevent heart disease, dementia, and bone loss. Further studies revealed in 2002 that HRT increases the risk of breast cancer, and, as the number of women taking it dropped sharply in the wake of this news, so did the incidence of breast cancer. So bad science may have produced the cancer in the first place, just as the bad science of positive thinking plagued me throughout my illness.

Breast cancer, I can now report, did not make me prettier or stronger, more feminine or spiritual. What it gave me, if you want to call this a "gift," was a very personal, agonizing encounter with an ideological force in American culture that I had not been aware of before—one that encourages us to deny reality, submit cheerfully to misfortune, and blame only ourselves for our fate.

TWO

The Years of Magical Thinking

Exhortations to think positively—to see the glass half full, even when it lies shattered on the floor—are not restricted to the pink ribbon culture of breast cancer. A few years after my treatment, I ventured out into another realm of personal calamity—the world of laid-off white-collar workers. At the networking groups, boot camps, and motivational sessions available to the unemployed, I found unanimous advice to abjure anger and "negativity" in favor of an upbeat, even grateful approach to one's immediate crisis. People who had been laid off from their jobs and were spiraling down toward poverty were told to see their condition as an "opportunity" to be embraced, just as breast cancer is often depicted as a "gift." Here, too, the promised outcome was a kind of "cure": by being positive, a person might not only feel better during his or her job search, but actually bring it to a faster, happier, conclusion.

In fact, there is no kind of problem or obstacle for which positive thinking or a positive attitude has not been proposed as a cure.

Trying to lose weight? "Once you have made up your mind to lose weight," a site devoted to "The Positive Weight Loss Approach" tells us, "you should make that commitment and go into it with a positive attitude. . . . Think like a winner, and not a loser." Having trouble finding a mate? Nothing is more attractive to potential suitors than a positive attitude or more repellant than a negative one. A Web site devoted to dating tips (one of many) advises people engaged in Internet dating: "Write a profile or message with a negative attitude and you are bound to send potential suitors packing. A positive attitude on the other hand is attractive to virtually everyone." Similarly, "the best blind date tips boil down to two basic pieces of advice," we learn from another Web site. "Have a positive attitude, and keep an open mind." Women in particular should radiate positivity, not mentioning, for example, that their last boyfriend was a jerk or that they're dissatisfied with their weight. "You should remain positive at all times," counsels yet another site. "You should avoid complaining too much, seeing the negative in things, and allowing all this negativity to show. While it is important that you are yourself, and should remain true to that, being negative is never a way to go when it comes to socialization [meaning, perhaps, socializing]."

Need money? Wealth is one of the principal goals of positive thinking, and something we will return to again and again in this book. There are hundreds of self-help books expounding on how positive thinking can "attract" money—a method supposedly so reliable that you are encouraged to begin spending it now. Why has wealth eluded you so far? Practical problems like low wages, unemployment, and medical bills are mentioned only as potential "excuses." The real obstacle lies in your mind, which may harbor a subconscious revulsion for "filthy lucre" or a deeply buried resentment of the rich. A friend of mine, a chronically underemployed photographer, once engaged a "life coach" to improve his finances and was told to overcome his negative feelings about wealth and to always carry a twenty-dollar bill in his wallet "to attract more money."

Positive thoughts are even solicited for others, much like prayers. On an Internet site for teachers, a woman asks colleagues to "please think positive thoughts for my son-in-law," who had just been diagnosed with Stage IV brain cancer. Appearing on CNN, the father of a soldier missing in action in Iraq told viewers: "I would wish everybody out there to give your positive thoughts on this issue and to help us through this. And if everybody gives us their prayers and their positive thoughts, this stuff is doable. . . . I know the military are doing all they can to do whatever they can, and the positive thoughts are very important right now."[1] Positive thoughts notwithstanding, the soldier's body was found in the Euphrates River one week later.

Like a perpetually flashing neon sign in the background, like an inescapable jingle, the injunction to be positive is so ubiquitous that it's impossible to identify a single source. Oprah routinely trumpets the triumph of attitude over circumstance. A Google search for "positive thinking" turns up 1.92 million entries. At the Learning Annex, which offers how-to classes in cities like New York and Los Angeles, you'll find a smorgasbord of workshops on how to succeed in life by overcoming pessimism, accessing your inner powers, and harnessing the power of thought. A whole coaching industry has grown up since the mid-1990s, heavily marketed on the Internet, to help people improve their attitudes and hence, supposedly, their lives. For a fee on a par with what a therapist might receive, an unlicensed career or life coach can help you defeat the "negative self-talk"—that is, pessimistic thoughts—that impedes your progress.

Within America today, a positive outlook is not always entirely voluntary: those who do not reach out to embrace the ideology of positive thinking may find it imposed on them. Workplaces make conscious efforts to instill a positive outlook, with employers bring- ing in motivational speakers or distributing free copies of self- help books like the 2001 paperback mega–best seller *Who Moved My Cheese?*, which counsels an uncomplaining response to layoffs. Nursing homes famously brim over with artificial cheerfulness. As one resident complained: "The diminutives! The endearments! The idotic *we*'s. Hello, dear, how are we doing today? What's your name, dear? Eve? Shall we go into the dining room, Eve? Hi, hon, sorry to take so long. Don't we look nice today!"[2] Even the acad- emy, which one might think would be a safe haven for cranky misanthropes, is seeing the inroads of positive thinking. In early 2007, the administration of Southern Illinois University at Car- bondale, alarmed by a marketing study finding the faculty "pride- less," brought in a motivational speaker to convince the glum professors that "a positive attitude is vital for improving cus- tomer satisfaction," the "customers" being the students. It should be noted that only 10 percent of the faculty bothered to attend the session.[3]

But positive thinking is not just a diffuse cultural consensus, spread by contagion. It has its ideologues, spokespeople, preach- ers, and salespersons—authors of self-help books, motivational speakers, coaches, and trainers. In 2007, I ventured into one of their great annual gatherings, a convention of the National Speakers As- sociation, where members of the latter occupational groups came together for four days to share techniques, boast of their successes, and troll for new business opportunities. The setting, a waterfront hotel in downtown San Diego, was pleasantly touristic, the internal ambience engineered for a maximally positive effect. A plenary session in the main ballroom began with a ten-minute slide show of calendar-style photos—waterfalls, mountains, and wildflowers— accompanied by soothing music. Then a middle-aged blond woman in an Indian-type tunic came out and led the 1,700-member audience in "vocal toning." "Aaaah," she said, "aaah, aaah, aaah," inviting us to stand and chant along with her. Everyone joined in, obediently but not enthusiastically, suggesting some prior experience with this sort of exercise.

It was New Age meets middle-American business culture. You could pick up some crystals at the exhibition booths or attend a session on how to market your Web site. You could hone your meditation skills or get tips on finding a speakers agency. You could delve into "ancient wisdom"—the Upanishads, the Kabala, Freemasonry, and so on—or you could purchase a wheeled suitcase personalized with your name and Web site in large letters, the better to market yourself while strolling through airports. There was nothing remotely cultlike about the crowd, no visible signs of fanaticism or inner derangement. Business casual prevailed and, among the men, shaved heads greatly outnumbered ponytails.

The irrational exuberance, such as it was, all came from the podium. First up, among the keynote speakers, was the slender, energetic Sue Morter, described in the program as the head of a "multi-disciplined wellness center in Indianapolis." When the initial applause she receives "doesn't do it" for her, she orders the audience to stand and engage in a few minutes of rhythmic clapping to music. Thus primed, we are treated to a fifty-minute discourse, delivered without notes, on the "infinite power" we can achieve by resonating in tune with the universe, which turns out to have a frequency of ten cycles per second. When we are out of resonance, "we tend to overanalyze, plan, and have negative thoughts." The alternative to all this thinking and planning is to "be in the Yes!" When she comes to the end, Morter has the audience stand again. "Squeeze your hands together, think the thought Yes. Put your feet firmly on the planet. Think the thought Yes."

Best known among the keynoters was Joe ("Mr. Fire") Vitale, introduced as "the guru himself," who claims doctorates in both metaphysical science and marketing. Vitale, who looks like a slightly elongated Danny DeVito, offers the theme of "inspired marketing," and also love. "You are just incredible," he begins. "I love all of you. You are fantastic." He admits to being a "disciple of P. T. Barnum" and recounts some of the pranks he has used to gain attention— like a tongue-in-cheek press release accusing Britney Spears of plagiarizing his "hypnotic marketing" techniques. Love seems to be among these techniques, since he recommends increasing one's business by looking over one's mailing list and "loving each name." He plugs his most recent book, *Zero Limits: The Secret Hawaiian System for Wealth, Health, Power, and More*, which explains how a doctor cured inmates in an asylum for the criminally insane without even seeing them, by simply studying their records and working to overcome his negative thoughts about them. Again, there is a jubilant finale: "Say 'I love you' in your head at all times so that we can heal all that needs to be healed."

The audience absorbs all this soberly, taking notes, nodding occasionally, laughing at the expected points. As far as I can judge, most of the attendees have not published books or ever addressed an audience as large as the National Speakers Association provides. Random conversations suggest that the majority are only wannabe speakers—coaches or trainers who aspire to larger audiences and fees. Many come from health-related fields, especially of the "holistic" or alternative variety; some are coaches for businesspeople, like the ones I had encountered instructing laid-off white-collar workers; a few are members of the clergy, seeking to expand their careers. Hence the predominance of workshops on nuts-and-bolts themes: how to work with speakers bureaus, acquire bookings, organize your office, market your "products" (DVDs and inspirational tapes). Not everyone will make it, as one work-

shop leader warns in her PowerPoint presentation, with a kind
of realism that seems sorely out of place. Some, she says, will go
into a "death spiral," spending more and more to market their
Web sites and their products, and "then—nothing." But clearly
there is money to be made. In one workshop, Chris Widener, a
forty-one-year-old motivational speaker who began as a minister, tells the story of his unpromising youth—he had been "out
of control" at the age of thirteen—culminating in his present
affluence: "Three and a half years ago, I bought my dream house
in the Cascade Mountains. It has a weight-lifting room, a wine
cellar, and a steam bath. . . . My life is what I would consider the
definition of success."

As fresh people advance in their speaking careers, what will be
their message, the content of their speeches? No one ever answered this question or, as far as I know, raised it at the NSA convention, I think because the answer is obvious: they will give
speeches much like those given here, insisting that the only barriers to health and prosperity lie within oneself. If you want to improve your life—both materially and subjectively—you need to
upgrade your attitude, revise your emotional responses, and focus your mind. One could think of other possible means of self-
improvement—through education, for example, to acquire new
"hard" skills, or by working for social changes that would benefit
all. But in the world of positive thinking, the challenges are all
interior and easily overcome through an effort of the will. This is
no doubt what freshly minted speakers will tell the audiences they
manage to find: *I too was once lost and overcome by self-doubt, but
then I found the key to success, and look at me now!* Some listeners
will learn by example that there is a career to be made proselytiz-
ing for positive thinking and will end up doing so themselves,
becoming new missionaries for the cult of cheerfulness.

The Menace of Negative People

The promise of positivity is that it will improve your life in concrete, material ways. In one simple, practical sense, this is probably true. If you are "nice," people will be more inclined to like you than if you are chronically grumpy, critical, and out of sorts. Much of the behavioral advice offered by the gurus, on their Web sites and in their books, is innocuous. "Smile," advises one success-oriented positive-thinking site. "Greet coworkers." The rewards for exuding a positive manner are all the greater in a culture that expects no less. Where cheerfulness is the norm, crankiness can seem perverse. Who would want to date or hire a "negative" person? What could be wrong with him or her? The trick, if you want to get ahead, is to simulate a positive outlook, no matter how you might actually be feeling.

The first great text on how to *act* in a positive way was Dale Carnegie's *How to Win Friends and Influence People*, originally published in 1936 and still in print. Carnegie—who was born Carnagey but changed his name apparently to match that of the industrialist Andrew Carnegie—did not assume that his readers *felt* happy, only that they could manipulate others by putting on a successful act: "You don't feel like smiling? Then what? Two things. First, force yourself to smile. If you are alone, force yourself to whistle or hum a tune or sing." You could "force" yourself to act in a positive manner, or you could be trained: "Many companies train their telephone operators to greet all callers in a tone of voice that radiates interest and enthusiasm." The operator doesn't have to feel this enthusiasm; she only has to "radiate" it. The peak achievement, in *How to Win Friends,* is to learn how to fake sincerity: "A show of interest, as with every other principle of human relationships, must be sincere."[4] How do you put on a "show" of sincerity? This is not explained, but it is hard to imagine succeeding at it without developing some degree of skill as an actor. In a famous study in the 1980s, sociologist Arlie Hochschild found that flight attendants became stressed and emotionally depleted by the requirement that they be cheerful to passengers at all times.[5] "They lost touch with their own emotions," Hochschild told me in an interview.

As the twentieth century wore on, the relevance of Carnegie's advice only increased. More and more middle-class people were not farmers or small business owners but employees of large corporations, where the objects of their labor were likely to be not physical objects, like railroad tracks or deposits of ore, but other people. The salesman worked on his customers; the manager worked on his subordinates and coworkers. Writing in 1956, sociologist William H. Whyte viewed this development with grave misgivings, as a step toward the kind of spirit-crushing collectivization that prevailed in the Soviet Union: "Organizational life being what it is, out of sheer necessity, [a man] must spend most of his working hours in one group or another." There were "the people at the conference table, the workshop, the seminar, the skull session, the after-hours discussion group, the project team." In this thickly peopled setting, the "soft skills" of interpersonal relations came to count for more than knowledge and experience in getting the job done. Carnegie had observed that "even in such technical lines as engineering, about 15 percent of one's financial success is due to one's technical knowledge and about 85 percent is due to skill in human engineering."[6]

Today, hardly anyone needs to be reminded of the importance of interpersonal skills. Most of us work with people, on people, and around people. We have become the emotional wallpaper in other people's lives, less individuals with our own quirks and needs than dependable sources of smiles and optimism. "Ninety-nine out of every 100 people report that they want to be around more positive people," asserts the 2004 self-help book *How Full Is Your Bucket? Positive Strategies for Work and Life*.[7] The choice seems obvious—critical and challenging people or smiling yes-sayers? And the more entrenched the cult of cheerfulness becomes, the more advisable it is to conform, because your coworkers will expect nothing less. According to human resources consultant Gary S. Topchik, "the Bureau of Labor Statistics estimates that U.S. companies lose $3 billion a year to the effects of negative attitudes and behaviors at work" through, among other things, lateness, rudeness, errors, and high turnover.[8] Except in clear-cut cases of racial, gender, age, or religious discrimination, Americans can be fired for anything, such as failing to generate positive vibes. A computer technician in Minneapolis told me he lost one job for uttering a stray remark that was never identified for him but taken as evidence of sarcasm and a "negative attitude." Julie, a reader of my Web site who lives in Austin, Texas, wrote to tell me of her experience working at a call center for Home Depot:

> I worked there for about a month when my boss pulled me into a small room and told me I "obviously wasn't happy enough to be there." Sure, I was sleep deprived from working five other jobs to pay for private health insurance that topped $300 a month and student loans that kicked in at $410 a month, but I can't recall saying anything to anyone outside the lines of "I'm happy to have a job." Plus, I didn't realize anyone had to be happy to work in a call center. My friend who works in one refers to it [having to simulate happiness] as the kind of feeling you might get from getting a hand job when your soul is dying.

What has changed, in the last few years, is that the advice to at least act in a positive way has taken on a harsher edge. The penalty for nonconformity is going up, from the possibility of job loss and failure to social shunning and complete isolation. In his 2005 best seller, *Secrets of the Millionaire Mind*, T. Harv Eker, founder of "Peak Potentials Training," advises that negative people have to go, even, presumably, the ones that you live with: "Identify a situation or a person who is a downer in your life. Remove yourself from that situation or association. If it's family, choose to be around them less."[9] In fact, this advice has become a staple of the self-help literature, of both the secular and Christian varieties. "GET RID OF NEGATIVE PEOPLE IN YOUR LIFE," writes motivational speaker and coach Jeffrey Gitomer. "They waste your time and bring you down. If you can't get rid of them (like a spouse or a boss), reduce your time with them."[10] And if that isn't clear enough, J. P. Maroney, a motivational speaker who styles himself "the Pitbull of Business," announces:

> Negative People SUCK!
> That may sound harsh, but the fact is that negative people do suck. They suck the energy out of positive people like you and me. They suck the energy and life out of a good company, a good team, a good relationship. . . . Avoid them at all cost. If you have to cut ties with people you've known for a long time because they're actually a negative drain on you, then so be it. Trust me, you're better off without them.[11]

What would it mean in practice to eliminate all the "negative people" from one's life? It might be a good move to separate from a chronically carping spouse, but it is not so easy to abandon the whiny toddler, the colicky infant, or the sullen teenager. And at the workplace, while it's probably advisable to detect and terminate those who show signs of becoming mass killers, there are other annoying people who might actually have something useful to say: the financial officer who keeps worrying about the bank's subprime mortgage exposure or the auto executive who questions the company's overinvestment in SUVs and trucks. Purge everyone who "brings you down," and you risk being very lonely or, what is worse, cut off from reality. The challenge of family life, or group life of any kind, is to keep gauging the moods of others, accommodating to their insights, and offering comfort when needed.

But in the world of positive thinking other people are not there to be nurtured or to provide unwelcome reality checks. They are there only to nourish, praise, and affirm. Harsh as this dictum sounds, many ordinary people adopt it as their creed, displaying wall plaques or bumper stickers showing the word "Whining" with a cancel sign through it. There seems to be a massive empathy deficit, which people respond to by withdrawing their own. No one has the time or patience for anyone else's problems.

In mid-2006, a Kansas City pastor put the growing ban on "negativity" into practice, announcing that his church would now be "complaint free." Also, there would be no criticizing, gossiping, or sarcasm. To reprogram the congregation, the Reverend Will Bowen distributed purple silicone bracelets that were to be worn as reminders. The goal? Twenty-one complaint-free days, after which the complaining habit would presumably be broken. If the wearer broke down and complained about something, then the bracelet was to be transferred to the other wrist. This bold attack on negativity brought Bowen a spread in *People* magazine and a spot on the *Oprah Winfrey Show*. Within a few months, his church had given out 4.5 million purple bracelets to people in over eighty countries. He envisions a complaint-free world and boasts that his bracelets have been distributed within schools, prisons, and homeless shelters. There is no word yet on how successful they have been in the latter two settings.

So the claim that acting in a positive way leads to success becomes self-fulfilling, at least in the negative sense that not doing so can lead to more profound forms of failure, such as rejection by employers or even one's fellow worshipers. When the gurus advise dropping "negative" people, they are also issuing a warning: smile and be agreeable, go with the flow—or prepare to be ostracized.

It is not enough, though, to cull the negative people from one's immediate circle of contacts; information about the larger human world must be carefully censored. All the motivators and gurus of positivity agree that it is a mistake to read newspapers or watch the news. An article from an online dating magazine offers, among various tips for developing a positive attitude: "Step 5: Stop Watching the News. Murder. Rape. Fraud. War. Daily news is often filled with nothing but negative stories and when you make reading such material a part of your daily lifestyle, you begin to be directly affected by that environmental factor."

Jeffrey Gitomer goes further, advising a retreat into one's personal efforts to achieve positive thinking: "All news is negative. Constant exposure to negative news can't possibly have a positive impact on your life. The Internet will give you all the news you need in about a minute and a half. That will free up time that you can devote to yourself and your positive attitude."[12]

Why is all news "negative"? Judy Braley, identified as an author and attorney, attributes the excess of bad news to the inadequate spread of positive thinking among the world's population:

> The great majority of the population of this world
> does not live life from the space of a positive attitude.
> In fact, I believe the majority of the population of
> this world lives from a place of pain, and that people

who live from pain only know how to spread more
negativity and pain. For me, this explains many of
the atrocities of our world and the reason why we are
bombarded with negativity all the time.[13]

At the NSA convention, I found myself talking to a tall man
whose shaved head, unsmiling face, and stiff bearing suggested
a military background. I asked him whether, as a coach, he felt
people needed a lot of pumping up because they were chronically
depressed. No, was his answer, sometimes they're just lazy. But
he went on to admit that he, too, got depressed when he read
about the war in Iraq, so he now scrupulously avoids the news.
"What about the need to be informed in order to be a responsible
citizen?" I asked. He gave me a long look and then suggested,
sagely enough, that this is what I should work on motivating
people to do.

For those who need more than the ninety-second daily up-
dates permitted by Gitomer, there are at least two Web sites offering nothing but "positive news." One of them, Good News Blog,
explains that "with ample media attention going out to the cruel,
the horrible, the perverted, the twisted, it is easy to become convinced that human beings are going down the drain. 'Good News'
was going to show site visitors that bad news is news simply because it *is* rare and unique." Among this site's recent top news
stories were "Adoptee Reunited with Mother via Webcam Reality
Show," "Students Help Nurse Rescued Horses Back to Good Health,"
and "Parrot Saves Girl's Life with Warning." At happynews.com,
there was a surprising abundance of international stories, although
not a word about Darfur, Congo, Gaza, Iraq, or Afghanistan. Instead, in a sampling of a day's offerings, I found "Seven-Month-
Old from Nepal Receives Life-Saving Surgery," "100th Anniversary
of the US-Canada Boundary Waters Treaty," "Many Americans

Making Selfless Resolutions," and "Childhood Sweethearts Attempt Romantic Adventure."

This retreat from the real drama and tragedy of human events is suggestive of a deep helplessness at the core of positive thinking. Why not follow the news? Because, as my informant at the NSA meeting told me, "You can't do anything about it." Braley similarly dismisses reports of disasters: "That's negative news that can cause you emotional sadness, but that you can't do anything about." The possibilities of contributing to relief funds, joining an antiwar movement, or lobbying for more humane government policies are not even considered. But at the very least there seems to be an acknowledgment here that no amount of attitude adjustment can make good news out of headlines beginning with "Civilian casualties mount . . ." or "Famine spreads . . ."

Of course, if the powers of mind were truly "infinite," one would not have to eliminate negative people from one's life either; one could, for example, simply choose to interpret their behavior in a positive way—maybe he's criticizing me for my own good, maybe she's being sullen because she likes me so much and I haven't been attentive, and so on. The advice that you must change your environment—for example, by eliminating negative people and news—is an admission that there may in fact be a "real world" out there that is utterly unaffected by our wishes. In the face of this terrifying possibility, the only "positive" response is to withdraw into one's own carefully constructed world of constant approval and affirmation, nice news, and smiling people.

The Law of Attraction

If ostracism is the stick threatening the recalcitrant, there is also an infinitely compelling carrot: think positively, and positive things will come to you. You can have anything, anything at all, by focusing your mind on it—limitless wealth and success, loving relationships, a coveted table at the restaurant of your choice. The universe exists to do your bidding, if only you can learn to harness the power of your desires. Visualize what you want and it will be "attracted" to you. "Ask, believe, and receive," or "Name it and claim it."

This astonishingly good news has been available in the United States for over a century, but it hit the international media with renewed force in late 2006, with the runaway success of a book and DVD entitled *The Secret*. Within a few months of publication, 3.8 million copies were in print, with the book hitting the top of both the *USA Today* and *New York Times* best seller lists. It helped that the book was itself a beautiful object, printed on glossy paper and covered in what looked like a medieval manuscript adorned with a red seal, vaguely evoking that other bestseller *The Da Vinci Code*. It helped also that the author, an Australian TV producer named Rhonda Byrne, or her surrogates won admiring interviews on *Oprah*, the *Ellen DeGeneres Show*, and *Larry King Live*. But *The Secret* relied mostly on word-of-mouth, spreading "like the Norwalk virus through Pilates classes, get-rich-quick websites and personal motivation blogs," as the *Ottawa Citizen* reported.[14] I met one fan, a young African American woman, in the bleak cafeteria of the community college she attends, where she confided that it was now *her* secret.

Despite its generally respectful media reception, *The Secret* attracted—no doubt unintentionally, in this case—both shock and ridicule from Enlightenment circles. The critics barely knew where to begin. In the DVD, a woman admires a necklace in a store window and is next shown wearing it around her neck, simply through her conscious efforts to "attract" it. In the book, Byrne, who struggled with her weight for decades, asserts that food does not make you fat—only the *thought* that food could make you fat actually results in weight gain. She also tells the story of a woman who "attracted" her perfect partner by pretending he was already with her: she left a space for him in her garage and cleared out her closets to make room for his clothes, and, lo, he came into her life.[15] Byrne herself claims to have used "the secret" to improve her eyesight and to no longer need glasses. Overwhelmed by all this magic, *Newsweek* could only marvel at the book's "explicit claim . . . that you can manipulate objective physical reality—the numbers in a lottery drawing, the actions of other people who may not even know you exist—through your thoughts and feelings."[16]

But Byrne was not saying anything new or original. In fact, she had merely packaged the insights of twenty-seven inspirational thinkers, most of them still living and many of them—like Jack Canfield, a coauthor of *Chicken Soup for the Soul*—already well known. About half the space in the book is taken up by quotes from these gurus, who are generously acknowledged as "featured co-authors" and listed with brief bios at the end. Among them are a "feng shui master," the president of a company selling "inspirational gifts," a share trader, and two physicists. But the great majority of her "co-authors" are people who style themselves as "coaches" and motivational speakers, including Joe Vitale, whose all-encompassing love I had experienced at the NSA meeting. The "secret" had hardly been kept under wraps; it was the collective wisdom of the coaching profession. My own first exposure to the mind-over-matter philosophy of *The Secret* had come three years before that book's publication, from a less than successful career coach in Atlanta, who taught that one's external conditions, such as failure and unemployment, are projections of one's "inner sense of well-being."

The notion that people other than athletes might need something called "coaching" arose in the 1980s when corporations began to hire actual sports coaches as speakers at corporate gatherings. Many salesmen and managers had played sports in school and were easily roused by speakers invoking crucial moments on the gridiron. In the late 1980s, John Whitmore, a former car racer and sports coach, carried coaching off the playing fields and into the executive offices, where its goal became to enhance "performance" in the abstract, including the kind that can be achieved while sitting at a desk. People who might formerly have called themselves "consultants" began to call themselves "coaches" and to set up shop to instill ordinary people, usually white-collar corporate employees, with a "winning" or positive attitude. One of the things the new coaches brought from the old world of sports coaching was the idea of visualizing victory, or at least a credible performance, before the game, just as Byrne and her confederates urge people to visualize the outcomes they desire.

Sports was only one source of the new wisdom, which had been bubbling up for years from the world of self-help gurus and "spiritual teachers," most of them not referenced by Byrne. For example, there was the 2004 docudrama *What the Bleep Do We Know?*, produced by a New Age sect led by a Tacoma woman named JZ Knight, who channels a 35,000-year-old warrior spirit named Ramtha. In the film, actor Marlee Matlin gives up Xanax for a spiritual appreciation of life's limitless possibilities. At the Ramtha School of Enlightenment, students write down their goals, post them on a wall, and attempt to realize them through strenuous forms of "meditation" involving high-decibel rock music. On the more businesslike side, "success coach" Mike Hernacki published his book *The Ultimate Secret to Getting Absolutely Everything You Want* in 1982; the genre continued with, among others, Michael J. Losier's 2006 book, *Law of Attraction: The Science of Attracting More of What You Want and Less of What You Don't*. T. Harv Eker's *Secrets of the Millionaire Mind* explains that "the universe, which is another way of saying 'higher power,' is akin to a big mail order department," an image also employed by Vitale.[17] If you send in your orders clearly and unambiguously, fulfillment is guaranteed in a timely fashion.

What attracts the coaching profession to these mystical powers? Well, there's not much else for them to impart to their coachees. "Career coaches" may teach their clients how to write résumés and deliver the self-advertisements known as "elevator speeches," but they don't have anything else by way of concrete skills to offer. Neither they nor more generic "success coaches" will help you throw a javelin farther, upgrade your computer skills, or manage the flow of information through a large department. All they can do is work on your attitude and expectations, so it helps to start with the metaphysical premise that success is guaranteed through some kind of attitudinal intervention. And if success does not follow, if you remain strapped for funds or stuck in an unpromising job, it's not the coach's fault, it's yours. You just didn't try hard enough and obviously need more work.

The metaphysics found in the coaching industry and books like *The Secret* bears an unmistakable resemblance to traditional folk forms of magic, in particular "sympathetic magic," which operates on the principle that like attracts like. A fetish or talisman—or, in the case of "black magic," something like a pinpricked voodoo doll—is thought to bring about some desired outcome. In the case of positive thinking, the positive thought, or mental image of the desired outcome, serves as a kind of internal fetish to hold in your mind. As religious historian Catherine Albanese explains, "In material magic, symbolic behavior involves the use of artifacts and stylized accoutrements, in ritual, or ceremonial, magic," while in "mental magic," of the positive-thinking variety, "the field is internalized, and the central ritual becomes some form of meditation or guided visualization."[18]

Sometimes, though, an actual physical fetish may be required. John Assaraf, an entrepreneur and coach featured in *The Secret*, explains the use of "vision boards":

> Many years ago, I looked at another way to represent some of the materialistic things I wanted to achieve in my life, whether it was a car or a house or anything. And so I started cutting out pictures of things that I wanted. And I put those vision boards up. And every day for probably about just two to three minutes, I would sit in [*sic*] my desk and I would look at my board and I'd close my eyes. And I'd see myself having the dream car and the dream home and the money in the bank that I wanted and the money that I wanted to have for charity.[19]

The link to older, seemingly more "primitive" forms of magic is unabashed in one Web site's instructions for creating a kind of vision board:

> Leaving the four corners of the card (posterboard) blank, decorate the rest of the face with glitter, ribbons, magical symbols, herbs, or any other items linked with the attributes of prosperity. Next, take the dollar bill and cut off the four corners. Glue the bill's triangular corners to the four corners of your card. This is sympathetic magic—one must have money to attract money. Then either on the back of the card or on a separate piece of paper, write out these instructions for using the talisman:
>
> This is a talisman of prosperity. Place it where you will see it every day, preferably in a bedroom.
>
> At least once a day hold it to your heart and spend

several minutes reciting the chant: talisman of prosperity, All good things come to me.
     Notice the magic begin.[20]

Homemade talismans aside, most coaches would be chagrined
by any association with magic. What gives positive thinking some
purchase on mainstream credibility is its claim to be based firmly
on science. Why do positive thoughts attract positive outcomes?
Because of the "law of attraction," which operates as reliably as
the law of gravity. Bob Doyle, one of the "featured co-authors" of
The Secret and founder of the "Wealth Beyond Reason" training
system, asserts on his Web site: "Contrary to mainstream thinking, the Law of Attraction is NOT a 'new-age' concept. It is a
scientific principle that absolutely is at work in your life right now."
The claims of a scientific basis undoubtedly help account for positive thinking's huge popularity in the business world, which might
be more skittish about an ideology derived entirely from, say, spirit
channeling or Rosicrucianism. And science probably helped attract major media attention to *The Secret* and its spokespeople, a
panel of whom were introduced by the poker-faced Larry King
with these words: "Tonight, unhappy with your love, your job,
your life, not enough money? Use your head. You can think yourself into a lot better you. Positive thoughts can transform, can attract the good things you know you want. Sound far-fetched?
Think again. It's supported by science."
     Coaches and self-help gurus have struggled for years to find a
force that could draw the desired results to the person who desires
them or a necklace in a store window to an admirer's neck. In his
1982 book, Hernacki settled on the familiar force of gravity, offering the equation linking the mass of two objects to their accelera-
tion. But even those whose science educations stopped at ninth
grade might notice some problems with this. One, thoughts are

not objects with mass; they are patterns of neuronal firing within the brain. Two, if they were exerting some sort of gravitational force on material objects around them, it would be difficult to take off one's hat.

In an alternative formulation offered by Michael J. Losier, the immaterial nature of thoughts is acknowledged; they become "vibrations." "In the vibrational world," he writes, "there are two kinds of vibrations, positive (+) and negative (-). Every mood or feeling causes you to emit, send-out or offer a vibration, whether positive or negative."[21] But thoughts are not "vibrations," and known vibrations, such as sound waves, are characterized by amplitude and frequency. There is no such thing as a "positive" or "negative" vibration.

Magnetism is another force that has long lured positive thinkers, going back to the 1937—and still briskly selling—*Think and Grow Rich!*, which declared that "thoughts, like magnets, attract to us the forces, the people, the circumstances of life which harmonize with [them]." Hence the need to "magnetize our minds with intense DESIRE for riches."[22] Now, as patterns of neuronal firing that produce electrical activity in the brain, thoughts do indeed generate a magnetic field, but it is a pathetically weak one. As *Scientific American* columnist Michael Shermer observes, "The brain's magnetic field of 10 [to the minus 15th power] tesla quickly dissipates from the skull and is promptly swamped by other magnetic sources, not to mention the earth's magnetic field of 10 [to the minus 5th power] tesla, which overpowers it by 10 orders of magnitude!" Ten orders of magnitude—or a ratio of 10,000,000,000 to one. As everyone knows, ordinary magnets are not attracted or repelled by our heads, nor are our heads attracted to our refrigerators.[23]

There does exist one way for mental activity to affect the physical world, but only with the intervention of a great deal of technology. Using biofeedback techniques, a person can learn, through pure trial and error, to generate brain electrical activity that can move a cursor on a computer screen. The person doing this must be wearing an electrode-studded cap, or electroencephalograph, to detect the electrical signals from inside the head, which are then amplified and sent to an interface with the computer, usually for the purpose of aiding a severely paralyzed person to communicate. No "mind over matter" forces are involved, except metaphorically, if the technology is taken as representing our collective "mind." A technologically unassisted person cannot move a computer cursor by thought alone, much less move money into his or her bank account.

Into this explanatory void came quantum physics, or at least a highly filtered and redacted version thereof. Byrne cites quantum physics in *The Secret,* as does the 2004 film *What the Bleep Do We Know?*, and today no cutting-edge coach neglects it. The great promise of quantum physics, to New Age thinkers and the philosophically opportunistic generally, is that it seems to release humans from the dull tethers of determinism. Anything, they imagine, can happen at the level of subatomic particles, where the familiar laws of Newtonian physics do not prevail, so why not in our own lives? Insofar as I can follow the reasoning, two features of quantum physics seem to offer us limitless freedom. One is the wave/particle duality of matter, which means that waves, like light, are also particles (photons) and that subatomic particles, like electrons, can also be understood as waves—that is, described by a wave equation. In the loony extrapolation favored by positive thinkers, whole humans are also waves or vibrations. "This is what we be," NSA speaker Sue Morter announced, wriggling her fingers to suggest a vibration, "a flickering," and as vibrations we presumably have a lot more freedom of motion than we do as gravity-bound, 150-or-so-pound creatures made of carbon, oxygen, and so forth.

Another, even more commonly abused notion from quantum physics is the uncertainty principle, which simply asserts that we cannot know both the momentum and position of a subatomic particle. In the more familiar formulation, we usually say that the act of measuring something at the quantum level affects what is being measured, since to measure the coordinates of a particle like an electron is to pin it down into a particular quantum state—putting it through a process known as "quantum collapse." In the fanciful interpretation of a New Agey physicist cited by Rhonda Byrne, "the mind is actually shaping the very thing that is being perceived."[24] From there it is apparently a short leap to the idea that we are at all times creating the entire universe with our minds. As one life coach has written: "We are Creators of the Universe. . . . With quantum physics, science is leaving behind the notion that human beings are powerless victims and moving toward an understanding that we are fully empowered creators of our lives and of our world."[25]

In the words of Nobel physicist Murray Gell-Mann, this is so much "quantum flapdoodle." For one thing, quantum effects come into play at a level vastly smaller than our bodies, our nerve cells, and even the molecules involved in the conduction of neuronal impulses. Responding to *What the Bleep Do We Know?*, which heavily invokes quantum physics to explain the law of attraction, the estimable Michael Shermer notes that "for a system to be described quantum-mechanically, its typical mass (m), speed (v) and distance (d) must be on the order of Planck's constant (h) [6.626×10^{-34} joule-seconds]," which is far beyond tiny. He cites a physicist's calculations "that the mass of neural transmitter molecules and their speed across the distance of the synapse are about two orders of magnitude too large for quantum effects to be influential."[26] In other words, even our thought processes seem to be stuck in the deterministic prison of classical Newtonian physics.

As for the mind's supposed power to shape the universe: if anything, quantum physics contains a humbling reminder of the *limits* of the human mind and imagination. The fact that very small things like electrons and photons can act like both waves and particles does not mean that they are free to do anything or, of course, that we can morph into waves ourselves. Sadly, what it means is that we cannot envision these tiny things, at least not with images derived from the everyday, nonquantum world. Nor does the uncertainty principle mean that "the mind is shaping the very thing that is being perceived," only that there are limits to what we can ever find out about, say, a quantum-level particle. Where is it "really" and how fast is it going? We cannot know. When contacted by *Newsweek*, even the mystically oriented physicists enlisted by Byrne in *The Secret* backed off from the notion of any physical force through which the mind can fulfill its desires.

But no such qualms dampened the celebration of quantum physics, or perhaps I should say "quantum physics," at the gathering of the NSA conference in San Diego. Sue Morter fairly bounded around the stage as she asserted that "your reality is simply determined by whatever frequency [of energy] you choose to dive into." Unfortunately, she added, "we've been raised in Newtonian thought," so it can be hard to grasp quantum physics. How much Morter, a chiropractor by profession, grasped was unclear; quite apart from the notion that we are vibrations choosing our own frequency, she made small annoying errors such as describing "the cloud of electrons around an atom." (Electrons are part of the atom, orbiting around its nucleus.) But the good news is that "science has shown without a shadow of a doubt" that we create our own reality. Somehow, the fact that particles can act like waves and vice versa means that "whatever you decide is true, is true"— an exceedingly hard proposition to debate.

After Morter's presentation, I went to a workshop entitled "The

Final Frontier: Your Unlimited Mind!," led by Rebecca Nagy, a
"wedding preacher" from Charlotte, North Carolina, who described herself as a member of the "quantum spiritual world." We
started by repeating after her, "I am a co-creator," with the prefix
"co" as an apparent nod to some other, more traditional form of
creator. Slide after slide went by, showing what appeared to be
planets with moons—or electrons?—in orbit around them or announcing that "human beings are both receivers and transmitters
of quantum (LIGHT ENERGY) signals." At one point Nagy called
for two volunteers to come to the front of the room to help illus-
trate the unlimited powers of mind. One of them was given two
dousing rods to hold and told to think of someone she loves. But
no matter how much Nagy fiddled with the position of the rods,
nothing happened, leading her to say, "No judgment here! Can we
agree on that? No judgment here!" Finally, after several more minutes of repositioning, she mumbled, "It ain't working," and suggested that this could be "because we're in a hotel."

I began to make it my business to see what other conference
goers thought of the inescapable pseudoscientific flapdoodle. They
were an outgoing lot, easy to strike up conversations with, and it
seemed to me that my doubts about the invocation of quantum
physics might get us past the level of "How are you enjoying the
conference?" to either some common ground or a grave intellectual rupture. Several modestly admitted that it went right over
their heads, but no one displayed the slightest skepticism. In one
workshop, I found myself sitting next to a woman who introduced
herself as a business professor. When I told her that I worried
about all the references to quantum physics, she said, "You're supposed to be shaken up here." No, I said, I was worried about what
it had to do with actual physics. "It's what I'm here for," she coun-
tered blandly. When I could come up with nothing more than a

"Huh?" she explained that quantum physics is "what's going to affect the global economy."

I did find one cynic—a workshop leader who had introduced himself as a "leadership coach" and "quantum physicist," though actually he claimed only a master's degree in nuclear physics. When I cornered him after the workshop, he allowed as how "there is some crap" but insisted that quantum physics and New Age thinking "overlap a lot." When I pushed harder, he told me that it wouldn't do any good to challenge the ongoing abuse of quantum physics, because "thousands of people believe it." But the most startling response I got to my quibbling came from an expensively dressed life coach from Southern California. After I summarized my discomfort with all the fake quantum physics in a couple of sentences, she gave me a kindly therapeutic look and asked, "You mean it doesn't work for you?"

I felt at that moment, and for the first time in this friendly crowd, absolutely alone. If science is something you can accept or reject on the basis of personal tastes, then what kind of reality did she and I share? If it "worked for me" to say that the sun rises in the west, would she be willing to go along with that, accepting it as my particular take on things? Maybe I should have been impressed that these positive thinkers bothered to appeal to science at all, whether to "vibrations" or quantum physics, and in however degraded a form. To base a belief or worldview on science or what passes for science is to reach out to the nonbelievers and the uninitiated, to say that they too can come to the same conclusions if they make the same systematic observations and inferences. The alternative is to base one's worldview on revelation or mystical insight, and these are things that cannot be reliably shared with others. In other words, there's something deeply sociable about science; it rests entirely on observations that can be shared with and repeated by others. But in a world where "everything you decide is true, is true," what kind of connection between people can there be? Science, as well as most ordinary human interaction, depends on the assumption that there are conscious beings other than ourselves and that we share the same physical world, with all its surprises, sharp edges, and dangers.

But it is not clear that there *are* other people in the universe as imagined by the positive thinkers or, if there are, that they matter. What if they want the same things that we do, like that necklace, or what if they hope for entirely different outcomes to, say, an election or a football game? In *The Secret* Byrne tells the story of Colin, a ten-year-old boy who was initially dismayed by the long waits for rides at Disney World. He had seen Byrne's movie, however, and knew it was enough to think the thought "Tomorrow I'd love to go on all the big rides and never have to wait in line." Presto, the next morning his family was chosen to be Disney's "First Family" for the day, putting them first in line and leaving "hundreds of families" behind them.[27] What about all those other children, condemned to wait because Colin was empowered by *The Secret*? Or, in the case of the suitor who was magically drawn to the woman who cleared out her closets and garage to make room for him, was this what he wanted for himself or was he only a pawn in her fantasy?

It was this latter possibility that finally provoked a reaction from Larry King the night he hosted a panel of *The Secret*'s "teachers." One of them said, "I've been master planning my life and one of the things that I actually dreamed of doing is sitting here facing you, saying what I'm about to say. So I know that it [the law of attraction] works." That was too much for King, who was suddenly offended by the idea of being an object of "attraction" in someone else's life. "If one of you have a vision board with my picture on it," he snapped, "I'll go to break." This was an odd situation for a famous talk show host—having to insist that he, Larry King, was not just an image on someone else's vision board but an independent being with a will of his own.

It's a glorious universe the positive thinkers have come up with, a vast, shimmering aurora borealis in which desires mingle freely with their realizations. Everything is perfect here, or as perfect as you want to make it. Dreams go out and fulfill themselves; wishes need only to be articulated. It's just a god-awful lonely place.

THREE

The Dark Roots
of American Optimism

Why did Americans, in such large numbers, adopt this uniquely sunny, self-gratifying view of the world? To some, the answer may be obvious: ours was the "new" world, overflowing with opportunity and potential wealth, at least once the indigenous people had been disposed of. Pessimism and gloom had no place, you might imagine, in a land that offered ample acreage to every settler squeezed out of overcrowded Europe. And surely the ever-advancing frontier, the apparently limitless space and natural resources, contributed to many Americans' eventual adoption of positive thinking as a central part of their common ideology. But this is not how it all began: Americans did not invent positive thinking because their geography encouraged them to do so but because they had tried the opposite.

The Calvinism brought by white settlers to New England could be described as a system of socially imposed depression. Its God was "utterly lawless," as literary scholar Ann Douglas has written, an all-powerful entity who "reveals his hatred of his creatures, not his love for them."[1] He maintained a heaven, but one with only limited seating, and those who would be privileged to enter it had been selected before their births through a process of predestination. The task for the living was to constantly examine "the loathsome abominations that lie in his bosom," seeking to uproot the sinful thoughts that are a sure sign of damnation.[2] Calvinism offered only one form of relief from this anxious work of self-examination, and that was another form of labor—clearing, planting, stitching, building up farms and businesses. Anything other than labor of either the industrious or spiritual sort—idleness or pleasure seeking—was a contemptible sin.

I had some exposure to this as a child, though in a diluted and nontheological form. One stream of my ancestors had fled Scotland when the landowners decided that their farms would be more profitably employed as sheep-grazing land, and they brought their harsh Calvinist Presbyterianism with them to British Columbia. Owing to a stint of extreme poverty in my grandmother's generation, my great-grandparents ended up raising my mother, and although she rebelled against her Presbyterian heritage in many ways—smoking, drinking, and reading such ribald texts as the Kinsey reports on human sexuality—she preserved some of its lineaments in our home. Displays of emotion, including smiling, were denounced as "affected," and tears were an invitation to slaps. Work was the only known antidote for psychic malaise, leaving my stay-at-home and only-high-school-educated mother to fill her time with fanatical cleaning and other domestic makework. "When you're down on your knees," she liked to say, "scrub the floor."

So I can appreciate some of the strengths instilled by the Calvinist spirit—or, more loosely, the Protestant ethic—such as the self-discipline and refusal to accept the imagined comfort of an

unconditionally loving God. But I also know something of its tor-
ments, mitigated in my case by my more Irish-derived father:
work—hard, productive, visible work in the world—was our only
prayer and salvation, both as a path out of poverty and as a refuge
from the terror of meaninglessness.

Elements of Calvinism, again without the theology, persisted
and even flourished in American culture well into the late twentieth century and beyond. The middle and upper classes came to
see busyness for its own sake as a mark of status in the 1980s and
1990s, which was convenient, because employers were demanding more and more of them, especially once new technologies
ended the division between work and private life: the cell phone is
always within reach; the laptop comes home every evening. "Multi-
tasking" entered the vocabulary, along with the new problem of
"workaholism." While earlier elites had flaunted their leisure, the
comfortable classes of our own time are eager to display evidence
of their exhaustion—always "in the loop," always available for a
conference call, always ready to go "the extra mile." In academia,
where you might expect people to have more control over their
workload hour by hour, the notion of overwork as virtue reaches
almost religious dimensions. Professors boast of being "crazed"
by their multiple responsibilities; summer break offers no vaca-
tion, only an opportunity for frantic research and writing. I once
visited a successful academic couple in their Cape Cod summer
home, where they proudly showed me how their living room had
been divided into his-and-her work spaces. Deviations from their
routine—work, lunch, work, afternoon run—provoked serious un-
ease, as if they sensed that it would be all too easy to collapse into
complete and sinful indolence.

In the American colonies—in New England and to a lesser
degree Virginia—it was the Puritans who planted this tough-
minded, punitive ideology. No doubt it helped them to survive in

the New World, where subsistence required relentless effort, but they also struggled to survive Calvinism itself. For the individual believer, the weight of Calvinism, with its demand for perpetual effort and self-examination to the point of self-loathing, could be unbearable. It terrified children, like the seventeenth-century judge Samuel Sewall's fifteen-year-old daughter, Betty. "A little after dinner," he reported, "she burst out into an amazing cry, which caused all the family to cry too. Her mother asked the reason. She gave none; at last said she was afraid she would go to hell, her sins were not pardoned."[3] It made people sick. In England, the early-seventeenth-century author Robert Burton blamed it for the epidemic of melancholy afflicting that nation:

> The main matter which terrifies and torments most
> that are troubled in mind is the enormity of their
> offences, the intolerable burthen of their sins, God's
> heavy wrath and displeasure so deeply apprehended
> that they account themselves . . . already damned. . . .
> This furious curiosity, needless speculation, fruitless
> meditation about election, reprobation, free will,
> grace . . . torment still, and crucify the souls of too
> many.[4]

Two hundred years later, this form of "religious melancholy" was still rampant in New England, often reducing formerly healthy adults to a condition of morbid withdrawal, usually marked by physical maladies as well as inner terror. George Beecher, for example—brother of Harriet Beecher Stowe—tormented himself over his spiritual status until he "shattered" his nervous system and committed suicide in 1843.[5]

Certainly early America was not the only place to tremble in what Max Weber called the "frost" of Calvin's Puritanism.[6] But it may be that conditions in the New World intensified the grip of this hopeless, unforgiving religion. Looking west, the early settlers saw not the promise of abundance, only "a hideous and desolate wilderness, full of wild beasts and wild men."[7] In the gloom of old-growth forests and surrounded by the indigenous "wild men," the settlers must have felt as hemmed in as they had been in crowded England. And if Calvinism offered no individual reassurance, it at least exalted the group, the congregation. You might not be saved yourself, but you were part of a social entity set apart by its rigorous spiritual discipline—and set above all those who were unclean, untamed, and unchurched.

In the early nineteenth century, the clouds of Calvinist gloom were just beginning to break. Forests were yielding to roads and eventually railroads. The native peoples slunk westward or succumbed to European diseases. With the nation rapidly expanding, fortunes could be made overnight, or just as readily lost. In this tumultuous new age of possibility, people of all sorts began to reimagine the human condition and reject the punitive religion of their forebears. Religious historian Robert Orsi emphasizes the speculative ferment of nineteenth-century American religious culture, which was "creatively alive with multiple possibilities, contradictions, tensions, concerning the most fundamental questions (the nature of God, the meaning of Christ, salvation, redemption, and so on)."[8] As Ralph Waldo Emerson challenged his countrymen: "Why should we grope among the dry bones of the past, or put the living generation into masquerade out of its faded wardrobe? The sun shines to-day also. There is more wool and flax in the fields. There are new lands, new men, new thoughts. Let us demand our own works and laws and worship."[9]

Not only philosophers were beginning to question their religious heritage. A substantial movement of workingmen, small farmers, and their wives used their meetings and publications to denounce "King-craft, Priest-craft, Lawyer-craft, and Doctor-craft" and insist on the primacy of individual judgment. One such person was Phineas Parkhurst Quimby, a self-educated watch-maker and inventor in Portland, Maine, who filled his journals with metaphysical ideas about what he called "the science of life and happiness"—the focus on happiness being itself an implicit reproach to Calvinism. At the same time, middle-class women were chafing against the guilt-ridden, patriarchal strictures of the old religion and beginning to posit a more loving, maternal deity. The most influential of these was Mary Baker, known to us today as Mary Baker Eddy—the daughter of a hardscrabble, fire-and-brimstone-preaching Calvinist farmer and, like Quimby, a self-taught amateur metaphysician. It was the meeting of Eddy and Quimby in the 1860s that launched the cultural phenomenon we now recognize as positive thinking.

As an intellectual tendency, this new, post-Calvinist way of thinking was called, generically enough, "New Thought" or the "New Thought movement." It drew on many sources—the tran-scendentalism of Emerson, European mystical currents like Swe-denborgianism, even a dash of Hinduism—and it seemed almost designed as a rebuke to the Calvinism many of its adherents had been terrified by as children. In the New Thought vision, God was no longer hostile or indifferent; he was a ubiquitous, all-powerful Spirit or Mind, and since "man" was really Spirit too, man was co-terminous with God. There was only "One Mind," infinite and all-encompassing, and inasmuch as humanity was a part of this universal mind, how could there be such a thing as sin? If it existed at all, it was an "error," as was disease, because if everything was Spirit or Mind or God, everything was actually perfect.

The trick, for humans, was to access the boundless power of Spirit and thus exercise control over the physical world. This thrilling possibility, constantly touted in today's literature on the "law of attraction," was anticipated by Emerson when he wrote that man "is learning the great secret, that he can reduce under his will, not only particular events, but great classes, nay the whole series of events, and so conform all facts to his character."[10]

New Thought might have remained in the realm of parlor talk and occasional lectures, except for one thing: the nineteenth century presented its adherents with a great practical test, which it passed with flying colors. In New Thought, illness was a disturbance in an otherwise perfect Mind and could be cured through Mind alone. Sadly, the strictly mental approach did not seem to work with the infectious diseases—such as diphtheria, scarlet fever, typhus, tuberculosis, and cholera—that ravaged America until the introduction of public sanitary measures at the end of the nineteenth century. But as Quimby and Eddy were to discover, it did work for the slow, nameless, debilitating illness that was reducing many middle-class Americans to invalidism.

The symptoms of this illness, which was to be labeled "neurasthenia" near the end of the century, were multitudinous and diffuse. According to one of her sisters, the teenage Mary Baker Eddy, for example, suffered from a "cankered" stomach and an "ulcer" on her lungs, "in addition to her former diseases."[11] Spinal problems, neuralgia, and dyspepsia also played a role in young Eddy's invalidism, along with what one of her doctors described as "hysteria mingled with bad temper."[12] Most sufferers, like Eddy, reported back problems, digestive ills, exhaustion, headaches, insomnia, and melancholy. Even at the time, there were suspicions, as there are today in the case of chronic fatigue syndrome, that the illness was not "real," that it was a calculated bid for attention and exemption from chores and social obligations. But we should recall that this was a time before analgesics, safe laxatives, or, of course, antidepressants, when the first prescription for any complaint, however counterproductively, was often prolonged bed rest.

Neurasthenia was hardly ever fatal, but to some observers it seemed every bit as destructive as the infectious diseases. Catharine Beecher, the sister of Harriet Beecher Stowe and poor George Beecher, traveled around the country and reported "a terrible decay of female health all over the land." Her field notes include the following: "Milwaukee, Wis. Mrs. A. frequent sick headaches. Mrs. B. very feeble. Mrs. S., well, except chills. Mrs. D., subject to frequent headaches. Mrs. B. very poor health. . . . Do not know one healthy woman in the place."[13] Women were not the only victims. William James, who was to become the founder of American psychology, lapsed into invalidism as a young man, as did George M. Beard, who later, as a physician, coined the term "neurasthenia." But the roster of well-known women who lost at least part of their lives to invalidism is impressive: Charlotte Perkins Gilman, who memorialized her experience with cruelly ineffective medical treatments in "The Yellow Wallpaper"; Jane Addams, the founder of the first settlement house; Margaret Sanger, the birth control crusader; Ellen Richards, the founder of domestic science; and Alice James, sister of William and Henry James. Catharine Beecher herself, one of the chroniclers of the illness, "suffered from hysteria and occasional paralytic afflictions."[14]

Without in any way impugning the motives of the afflicted, George M. Beard recognized that neurasthenia presented a very different order of problem from diseases like diphtheria, which, for the first time, were being traced to an external physical agent—microbes. Neurasthenia, as his term suggests, represented a malfunction of the nerves. To Beard, the ailment seemed to arise from the challenge of the new: some people simply could not cope with America's fast-growing, increasingly urban, and highly mobile society. Their nerves were overstrained, he believed; they collapsed.

But the invalidism crippling America's middle class had more to do with the grip of the old religion than the challenge of new circumstances. In some ways, the malady was simply a continuation of the "religious melancholy" Robert Burton had studied in England around the time when the Puritans set off for Plymouth. Many of the sufferers had been raised in the Calvinist tradition and bore its scars all their lives. Mary Baker Eddy's father, for example, had once been so incensed to find some children playing with a semitame crow on the Sabbath that he killed the bird with a rock on the spot. As a girl, Eddy agonized over the Calvinist doctrine of predestination to the point of illness: "I was unwilling to be saved, if my brothers and sisters were to be numbered among those who were doomed to perpetual banishment from God. So perturbed was I by the thoughts aroused by this erroneous doctrine, that the family doctor was summoned, and pronounced me stricken with fever."[15]

Similarly, Lyman Beecher, the father of Catharine and George, had urged them as young children to "agonize, *agonize*" over the condition of their souls and "regularly subjected their hearts to . . . scrutiny" for signs of sin or self-indulgence.[16] Charles Beard, a sufferer himself and the son of a strict Calvinist preacher, later condemned religion for teaching children that "to be happy is to be doing wrong."[17] Even those not raised in the Calvinist religious tradition had usually endured child-raising methods predicated on the notion that children were savages in need of discipline and correction—an approach that was to linger in American middle-class culture until the arrival of Benjamin Spock and "permissive" child-raising in the 1940s.

But there is a more decisive reason to reject the notion that the invalidism of the nineteenth century arose from nervous exhaustion in the face of overly rapid expansion and change. If Beard's hypothesis were true, you would expect the victims to be drawn primarily from the cutting edge of economic dynamism. Industrialists, bankers, prospectors in the Gold Rush of 1848 should have been swooning and taking to their beds. Instead, it was precisely the groups most excluded from the frenzy of nineteenth-century competitiveness that collapsed into invalidism—clergymen, for example. In this era—before megachurches and television ministries—they tended to lead somewhat cloistered and contemplative lives, often remaining within the same geographical area for a lifetime. And nineteenth-century clergymen were a notoriously sickly lot. Ann Douglas cites an 1826 report that "the health of a large number of clergymen has failed or is failing them"; they suffered from dyspepsia, consumption, and a "gradual wearing out of the constitution."[18]

The largest demographic to suffer from invalidism or neurasthenia was middle-class women. Male prejudice barred them from higher education and most of the professions; industrialization was stripping away the productive tasks that had occupied women in the home, from sewing to soapmaking. For many women, invalidism became a kind of alternative career. Days spent reclining on chaise longues, attended by doctors and family members and devoted to trying new medicines and medical regimens, substituted for "masculine" striving in the world. Invalidism even became fashionable, as one of Mary Baker Eddy's biographers writes: "Delicate ill-health, a frailty unsuited to labor, was coming to be considered attractive in the young lady of the 1830s and 1840s, and even in rural New Hampshire sharp young women like the Baker girls had enough access to the magazines and novels of their day to know the fashions."[19]

Here, too, under the frills and sickly sentimentality of nineteenth-century feminine culture, we can discern the claw marks of Calvinism. The old religion had offered only one balm for the tormented soul, and that was hard labor in the material world. Take that away and you were left with the morbid introspection that was so conducive to dyspepsia, insomnia, backaches, and all the other symptoms of neurasthenia. Fashionable as it may have been, female invalidism grew out of enforced idleness and a sense of uselessness, and surely involved genuine suffering, mental as well as physical. Alice James rejoiced when, after decades of invalidism, she was diagnosed with breast cancer and told she would be dead in a few months.

Among men, neurasthenia sometimes arose in a period of idleness associated with youthful indecision about a career, as happened in the case of George Beard. Similarly, William James was uncertain about his early choice of medicine when, at the age of twenty-four, his back went out while he was bent over a cadaver. Already suffering from insomnia, digestive troubles, and eye problems, he fell into a paralyzing depression. The medical profession seemed to him too unscientific and illogical, but he could think of nothing else, writing, "I shall hate myself until I get some special work."[20] Women had no "special work"; a clergyman's day-to-day labors were amorphous and overlapped with the kinds of things women normally did, like visiting the sick. Without real work— "special work"—the Calvinist or Calvinist-influenced soul consumed itself with self-loathing.

The mainstream medical profession had no effective help for the invalid, and a great many interventions that were actually harmful. Doctors were still treating a variety of symptoms by bleeding the patient, often with leeches, and one of their favorite remedies was the toxic, mercury-containing calomel, which could cause the jaw to rot away. In Philadelphia, one of America's most noted physicians treated female invalids with soft, bland foods and weeks of bed rest in darkened rooms—no reading or conversation allowed. The prevailing "scientific" view was that invalidism was natural and perhaps inevitable in women, that the mere fact of being female was a kind of disease, requiring as much medical intervention as the poor invalid's family could afford. Why men should also sometimes suffer was not clear, but they, too, were treated with bleedings, purges, and long periods of enforced rest.

Mainstream medicine's failure to relieve the epidemic of invalidism, and the tragic consequences of many of its interventions, left the field open to alternative sorts of healers. Here is where Phineas Parkhurst Quimby, usually considered the founder of the New Thought movement and hence grandfather of today's positive thinking, comes in. He had no use for the medical profession, considering it a source of more sickness than health. Having dabbled for some time in mesmerism—along with metaphysics and watchmaking—he went into practice as a healer himself in 1859. A fearless thinker, though by no means irreligious, he quickly identified Calvinism as the source of many of his patients' ills. As he saw it, according to historian Roy M. Anker, "old-style Calvinism depressed people, its morality constricted their lives and bestowed on them large burdens of debilitating, disease-producing, guilt."[21] Quimby gained a minor reputation with a kind of "talking cure," through which he endeavored to convince his patients that the universe was fundamentally benevolent, that they were one with the "Mind" out of which it was constituted, and that they could leverage their own powers of mind to cure or "correct" their ills.

In 1863, Mary Baker Eddy, forty-two, made the then-arduous journey to Portland to seek help from Quimby, arriving so weak that she had to be carried up the stairs to his consulting rooms.[22] Eddy had been an invalid since childhood and might have been happy to continue that lifestyle—doing a little reading and writing in her more vigorous moments—if anyone had been willing to finance it. But her first husband had died and the second had absconded, leaving her nearly destitute in middle age, reduced to moving from one boardinghouse to another, sometimes just in time to avoid paying the rent. Perhaps she was a bit smitten with the handsome, genial Quimby, and possibly the feelings were returned; Mrs. Quimby certainly distrusted the somewhat pretentious and overly needy new patient. Whatever went on between them, Eddy soon declared herself cured, and when Quimby died three years later, she claimed his teachings as her own— although it should be acknowledged that Eddy's followers still insist that she was the originator of the New Thought approach. Either way, Quimby proved that New Thought provided a practical therapeutic approach, which the prolific writer and charismatic teacher Mary Baker Eddy went on to promote.

Eddy eventually gained considerable wealth by founding her own religion—Christian Science, with its still ubiquitous "reading rooms." The core of her teaching was that there is no material world, only Thought, Mind, Spirit, Goodness, Love, or, as she often put it in almost economic terms, "Supply." Hence there could be no such things as illness or want, except as temporary delusions. Today, you can find the same mystical notion in the teachings of "coaches" like Sue Morter: the world is dissolved into Mind, Energy, and Vibrations, all of which are potentially subject to our conscious control. This is the "science" of Christian Science, much as "quantum physics" (or magnetism) is the "scientific" bedrock of positive thinking. But it arose in the nineteenth century as an actual religion, and in opposition to the Calvinist version of Christianity.

In the long run, however, the most influential convert to Quimby's New Thought approach to healing was not Mary Baker Eddy but William James, the first American psychologist and definitely a man of science. James sought help for his miscellaneous ills from another disciple—and former patient—of Quimby's, Annetta Dresser.[23] Dresser must have been successful, because in his best-known work, *The Varieties of Religious Experience*, James enthused over the New Thought approach to healing: "The blind have been made to see, the halt to walk. Life-long invalids have had their health restored."[24] To James, it did not matter that New Thought was a philosophical muddle; it *worked*. He took it as a tribute to American pragmatism that Americans' "only decidedly original contribution to the systematic philosophy of life"—New Thought—had established itself through "concrete therapeutics" rather than, say, philosophical arguments. New Thought had won its great practical victory. It had healed a disease—the disease of Calvinism, or, as James put it, the "morbidness" associated with "the old hell-fire theology."[25]

James understood that New Thought offered much more than a new approach to healing; it was an entirely new way of seeing the world, so pervasive, he wrote, that "one catches [the] spirit at second-hand":

> One hears of the "Gospel of Relaxation," of the "Don't Worry Movement," of people who repeat to themselves "Youth, health, vigor!" when dressing in the morning as their motto for the day. Complaints of the weather are getting to be forbidden in many households; and more and more people are recognizing it to be bad form to speak of disagreeable

sensations, or to make much of the ordinary incon-
veniences and ailments of life.[26]

As a scientist, he was repelled by much of the New Thought literature, finding it "so moonstruck with optimism and so vaguely
expressed that an academically trained mind finds it almost impossible to read at all." Still, he blessed the new way of thinking as
"healthy-mindedness" and quoted another academic to the effect
that it was "hardly conceivable" that so many intelligent people
would be drawn to Christian Science and other schools of New
Thought "if the whole thing were a delusion."[27]

By the early twentieth century, the rise of scientific medicine,
powered originally by the successes of the germ theory of disease,
began to make New Thought forms of healing seem obsolete.
Middle-class homemakers left their sickbeds to take up the challenge of fighting microbes within their homes, informed by Ellen
Richards's "domestic science." Teddy Roosevelt, assuming the presidency in 1901, exemplified a new doctrine of muscular activism
that precluded even the occasional nap. Of the various currents of
New Thought, only Christian Science clung to the mind-over-body
notion that all disease could be cured by "thought"; the results
were often disastrous, as even some late-twentieth-century adherents chose to read and reread Mary Baker Eddy rather than take
antibiotics or undergo surgery. More forward-looking advocates
of New Thought turned away from health and found a fresh field
as promoters of success and wealth. Not until the 1970s would
America's positive thinkers dare to reclaim physical illnesses—
breast cancer, for example—as part of their jurisdiction.

However "moonstruck" its central beliefs, positive thinking
came out of the nineteenth century with the scientific imprima-
tur of William James and the approval of "America's favorite phi-
losopher," Ralph Waldo Emerson. Writing in the mid-twentieth

century, Norman Vincent Peale, the man who popularized the phrase "positive thinking," cited them repeatedly, though not as often as he did the Bible. James, in particular, made positive thinking respectable, not because he found it intellectually convincing but because of its undeniable success in "curing" the poor invalid victims of Calvinism. There is a satisfying irony here: in fostering widespread invalidism, Calvinism had crafted the instrument of its own destruction. It had handed New Thought, or what was to be called positive thinking, a dagger to plunge into its own chest.

But wait, there is a final twist to the story. If one of the best things you can say about positive thinking is that it articulated an alternative to Calvinism, one of the worst is that it ended up preserving some of Calvinism's more toxic features—a harsh judgmentalism, echoing the old religion's condemnation of sin, and an insistence on the constant interior labor of self-examination. The American alternative to Calvinism was not to be hedonism or even just an emphasis on emotional spontaneity. To the positive thinker, emotions remain suspect and one's inner life must be subjected to relentless monitoring.

In many important ways, Christian Science itself never fully broke with Calvinism at all. Its twentieth-century adherents were overwhelmingly white, middle-class people of outstandingly temperate, even self-denying habits. The British writer V. S. Pritchett, whose father was a "Scientist," wrote that they "gave up drink, tobacco, tea, coffee—dangerous drugs—they gave up sex, and wrecked their marriages on this account. . . . It was notoriously a menopause religion."[28] In her later years, Mary Baker Eddy even brought back a version of the devil to explain why, in this perfect universe, things did not always go her way. Bad weather, lost objects, imperfect printings of her books—all these were attributed to "Malicious Animal Magnetism" emanating from her imagined enemies.

In my own family, the great-grandmother who raised my mother had switched from Presbyterianism to Christian Science at some point in her life, and the transition was apparently seamless enough for my grandmother to later eulogize her in a letter simply as "a good Christian woman." My own mother had no more interest in Christian Science than she did in Presbyterianism, but she hewed to one of its harsher doctrines—that, if illness was not entirely imaginary, it was something that happened to people weaker and more suggestible than ourselves. Menstrual cramps and indigestion were the fantasies of idle women; only a fever or vomiting merited a day off from school. In other words, illness was a personal failure, even a kind of sin. I remember the great trepidation with which I confessed to my mother that I was having trouble seeing the blackboard in school; *we* were not the sort of people who needed glasses.

But the most striking continuity between the old religion and the new positive thinking lies in their common insistence on *work*—the constant internal work of self-monitoring. The Calvinist monitored his or her thoughts and feelings for signs of laxness, sin, and self-indulgence, while the positive thinker is ever on the lookout for "negative thoughts" charged with anxiety or doubt. As sociologist Micki McGee writes of the positive-thinking self-help literature, using language that harks back to its religious antecedents, "continuous and never-ending work on the self is offered not only as a road to success but also to a kind of secular salvation."[29] The self becomes an antagonist with which one wrestles endlessly, the Calvinist attacking it for sinful inclinations, the positive thinker for "negativity." This antagonism is made clear in the common advice that you can overcome negative thoughts by putting a rubberband on your wrist: "Every time you have a negative thought stretch it out and let it snap. Pow. That hurts. It may even leave a welt if your rubber band is too thick. Take it easy, you aren't trying to maim yourself, but you are trying to create a little bit of a pain avoidance reflex with the negative thoughts."[30]

A curious self-alienation is required for this kind of effort: there is the self that must be worked on, and another self that does the work. Hence the ubiquitous "rules," work sheets, self-evaluation forms, and exercises offered in the positive-thinking literature. These are the practical instructions for the work of conditioning or reprogramming that the self must accomplish on itself. In the twentieth century, when positive thinkers had largely abandoned health issues to the medical profession, the aim of all this work became wealth and success. The great positive-thinking text of the 1930s, *Think and Grow Rich!* by Napoleon Hill, set out the familiar New Thought metaphysics. "Thoughts are things"—in fact, they are things that attract their own realization. "ALL IMPULSES OF THOUGHT HAVE A TENDENCY TO CLOTHE THEMSELVES IN THEIR PHYSICAL EQUIVALENT." Hill reassured his readers that the steps required to achieve this transformation of thoughts into reality would not amount to "hard labor," but if any step was omitted, *"you will fail!"* Briefly put, the seeker of wealth had to draw up a statement including the exact sum of money he or she intended to gain and the date by which it should come, which statement was to be read "aloud, twice daily, once just before retiring at night and once after arising in the morning." By strict adherence to this regimen, one could manipulate the "subconscious mind," as Hill called the part of the self that required work, into a "white heat of DESIRE for money." To further harness the subconscious mind to conscious greed, he advises at one point that one "READ THIS ENTIRE CHAPTER ALOUD ONCE EVERY NIGHT."[31]

The book that introduced most twentieth-century Americans— as well as people worldwide—to the ceaseless work of positive thinking was, of course, Norman Vincent Peale's 1952 *The Power of Positive Thinking.* Peale was a mainstream Protestant minister who had been attracted to New Thought early in his career, thanks, he later wrote, to a New Thought proponent named Ernest Holmes. "Only those who knew me as a boy," he wrote, "can fully appreciate what Ernest Holmes did for me. Why, he made me a positive thinker."[32] If Peale saw any conflict between positive thinking and the teachings of the Calvinist-derived Dutch Reformed Church that he eventually adopted as his denomination, it did not perturb him. A mediocre student, he had come out of divinity school with a deep aversion to theological debates—and determined to make Christianity "practical" in solving people's ordinary financial, marital, and business problems. Like the nineteenth-century New Thought leaders before him, he saw himself in part as a healer; only the twentieth-century illness was not neurasthenia but what Peale identified as an "inferiority complex," something he had struggled with in his own life. In one of his books, written well after the publication of his perennial best seller, *The Power of Positive Thinking,* he wrote:

> A man told me he was having a lot of trouble with himself. "You are not the only one," I reflected, thinking of the many letters I receive from people who ask for help with problems. And also thinking of myself; for I must admit that the person who has caused me the most trouble over the years has been Norman Vincent Peale. . . . If we are our own chief problem, the basic reason must be found in the type of thoughts which habitually occupy and direct our minds.[33]

We have seen the enemy, in other words, and it is ourselves, or at least our thoughts. Fortunately though, thoughts can be monitored and corrected until, to paraphrase historian Donald Meyer's summary of Peale, positive thoughts became "automatic" and the individual became fully "conditioned."[34] Today we might call this the work of "reprogramming," and since individuals easily lapse back into negativity—as Peale often noted with dismay—it had to be done again and again. In *The Power of Positive Thinking,* Peale offered "ten simple, workable rules," or exercises, beginning with:

1. Formulate and stamp indelibly on your mind a mental picture of yourself as succeeding. Hold this picture tenaciously. Never permit it to fade. Your mind will seek to develop this picture. . . .
2. Whenever a negative thought concerning your personal powers comes to mind, deliberately voice a positive thought to cancel it out.
3. Do not build up obstacles in your imagination. Depreciate every so-called obstacle. Minimize them.[35]

Peale trusted the reader to come up with his or her own positive thoughts, but over time the preachers of positivity have found it more and more necessary to provide a kind of script in the form of "affirmations" or "declarations." In *Secrets of the Millionaire Mind,* for example, T. Harv Eker offers the reader the following instructions in how to overcome any lingering resistance to the wealth he or she deserves:

> Place your hand on your heart and say . . .
> *"I admire rich people!"*
> *"I bless rich people!"*
> *"I love rich people!"*
> *"And I'm going to be one of those rich people too!"*[36]

This work is never done. Setbacks can precipitate relapses into negativity, requiring what one contemporary guru, M. Scott Peck, calls "a continuing and never-ending process of self-monitoring."[37] Or, more positively, endless work may be necessitated by constantly raising your sights. If you are satisfied with your current condition, you need to "sharpen the saw," in self-help writer Stephen Covey's words, and admit you could be doing better. As the famed motivator Tony Robbins puts it: "When you set a goal, you've committed to CANI [Constant, Never-Ending Improvement]! You've acknowledged the need that all human beings have for constant, never-ending improvement. There is a power in the pressure of dissatisfaction, in the tension of temporary discomfort. This is the kind of pain you *want* in your life."[38]

There is no more exhausting account of the self-work required for positive thinking than motivational speaker Jeffrey Gitomer's story of how he achieved and maintains his positive attitude. We last encountered Gitomer demanding a purge of "negative people" from one's associates, much as an old-style Calvinist might have demanded an expulsion of sinners, but Gitomer had not always been so self-confidently positive. In the early 1970s, his business was enjoying only "moderate success," his marriage was "bad," and his wife was pregnant with twins. Then he fell in with a marketing company called Dare to Be Great, whose founder now claims to have anticipated the 2006 best seller *The Secret* by thirty-five years. Told by his new colleagues that "you're going to get a positive attitude . . . and you're going to make big money. Go, go, go!" he sold his business and plunged into the work of self-improvement. He watched the motivational film *Challenge to America* over five times a week and obsessively reread Napoleon Hill's *Think and Grow Rich!* with his new colleagues: "Each person was responsible for writing and presenting a book report on one chapter each day. There were 16 chapters in the book, 10 people in the room, and we did this for one year. You can do the math for how many times I have read the book."[39] At first the best he could do was fake a positive attitude: "Friends would ask me how I was doing, and I would extend my arms into the air and scream, 'Great!' Even though I was crappy." Suddenly, "one day I woke up, and I had a positive attitude. . . . I GOT IT! I GOT IT!"[40]

Substitute the Bible for *Think and Grow Rich!* and you have a conversion tale every bit as dramatic as anything Christian lore has to offer. Like the hero of the great seventeenth-century Calvinist classic *The Pilgrim's Progress,* Gitomer had found himself trapped by family and wallowing in his slough of despond—of mediocrity, rather than sin—and like Bunyan's hero, Gitomer shook off his old business, and his first wife, in order to remake himself. Just as Calvinism demanded not only a brief experience of conversion but a lifetime of self-examination, Gitomer's positive attitude requires constant "maintenance," in the form of "reading something positive every morning, thinking positive thoughts every morning, . . . saying positive things every morning," and so forth.[41] This is work, and just to make that clear, Gitomer's *Little Gold Book of YES! Attitude* offers a photograph of the author in a blue repairman's shirt bearing the label "Positive Attitude Maintenance Department."

Reciting affirmations, checking off work sheets, compulsively rereading get-rich-quick books: these are not what Emerson had in mind when he urged his countrymen to shake off the shackles of Calvinism and embrace a bounteous world filled with "new lands, new men, and new thoughts." He was something of a mystic, given to moments of transcendent illumination: "I become a universal eyeball. I am nothing; I see all. . . . All mean egotism vanishes."[42] In such states, the self does not double into a worker and an object of work; it disappears. The universe cannot be "supply," since such a perception requires a desiring, calculating ego, and as soon as ego enters into the picture, the sense of Oneness is shattered. Transcendent Oneness does not require self-examination, self-help, or self-work. It requires self-loss.

Still, surely it is better to obsess about one's chances of success than about the likelihood of hell and damnation, to search one's inner self for strengths rather than sins. The question is why one should be so inwardly preoccupied at all. Why not reach out to others in love and solidarity or peer into the natural world for some glimmer of understanding? Why retreat into anxious introspection when, as Emerson might have said, there is a vast world outside to explore? Why spend so much time working on oneself when there is so much real work to be done?

From the mid-twentieth century on, there was an all too practical answer: more and more people were employed in occupations that seemed to require positive thinking and all the work of self-improvement and maintenance that went into it. Norman Vincent Peale grasped this as well as anyone: the work of Americans, and especially of its ever-growing white-collar proletariat, is in no small part work that is performed on the self in order to make that self more acceptable and even likeable to employers, clients, coworkers, and potential customers. Positive thinking had ceased to be just a balm for the anxious or a cure for the psychosomatically distressed. It was beginning to be an obligation imposed on all American adults.

FOUR

Motivating Business and the Business of Motivation

Today there is no excuse for remaining stuck in the swamp of negativity. A whole industry has grown up to promote positive thinking, and the product of this industry, available at a wide range of prices, is called "motivation." You can buy it in traditional book form, along with CDs and DVDs featuring the author, or you can opt for the more intense experience of being coached or of attending a weeklong "seminar." If you have the money, you might choose to go to a weekend session in an exotic locale with a heavy-hitting motivational speaker. Or you can consume motivation in its many inert, fetishized forms—posters and calendars, coffee mugs, and desk accessories, all emblazoned with inspirational messages. Successories, a company devoted entirely to motivational products, offers a line of "Positive Pals," including a "bean bag starfish" wearing a life preserver bearing the words "Reach for the Stars." Most recently, a canny retailer has invented the "Life

Is Good" line of products, including T-shirts, blankets, banners, luggage tags, dog collars, and tire covers.

It doesn't matter where you start shopping: one product tends to lead ineluctably to another. Motivational gurus write books in order to get themselves speaking engagements, which in turn become opportunities for selling the books and perhaps other products the guru is offering, some of them not obviously related to the quest for a positive attitude. Superstar motivational speaker Tony Robbins, for example, sells nutritional supplements on his Web site along with his books and at one point was heavily involved in marketing Q-Link, a pendant that supposedly protected the wearer from cell phone radiation. Many thousands of potential customers are drawn into the motivation market through the thirty "Get Motivated!" rallies held each year in various cities, at which, for a low ticket price of about fifty dollars, one can hear celebrity speakers like Colin Powell or Bill Cosby. Many things go on at the rallies—"platitudes, pep talks, canned-ham humor, live infomercials, prefab patriotism, Bible Belt Christianity," according to one newspaper report— but they serve largely as showcases for dozens of other products, including books, tapes, personal coaching, and further training in the art of positive thinking.[1] According to John LaRosa of Marketdata Enterprises Inc., which tracks the self-help industry, "basically the money is made in the back of the room, as they say," through the sale of "books and tapes and multimedia packages."[2]

Millions of individuals buy these products. People facing major illnesses are particularly susceptible, as are the unemployed and people in risky lines of work. In 2007, I got to know Sue Goodhart, a realtor who was showing me houses, and I happened to mention that I was doing some research on motivational speakers. She smiled ruefully and gestured toward the backseat of her car, which I saw was piled with motivational CDs. When I teased her for being a "motivation junkie," she told me that she'd come from a working-class background and had never been encouraged to set high goals for herself. Then, at some point in the 1990s, her agency brought in a motivational firm called the Pacific Institute, which provided a five-day session on "goal-setting, positive thinking, visualization, and getting out of your comfort zone," and she began to think of herself as a self-determining individual and potential success. But that first exposure was hardly enough. She continues to listen to motivational CDs in her car from house to house, both because "sales is a lonely business" and because the CDs help her get to "the next level."

But the motivation industry would not have become the multibillion-dollar business that it is if it depended entirely on individual consumers.* It carved out a much larger and more free-spending market, and that new market was business in general, including America's largest companies. Corporations buy motivational products in bulk—books by the thousands, for example—for free distribution to employees. They can pay for motivational speakers, who typically charge five-figure fees per gig and often more. Almost any major U.S. company can be found on the lists of clients proudly displayed on motivational speakers' Web sites; a book on the motivational-speaking business mentions Sprint,

---

* Marketdata Enterprises estimates that in 2005 the total U.S. market for "self-improvement products"—including tapes, books, and coaches on business, diet, and relationships—amounted to $9.6 billion, but with the caveat that "information about the market and its privately owned competitors is still very difficult to obtain. Most companies or organizations are very reluctant to give out any information regarding their revenues, enrollments at their programs, or how they are doing/how fast they are growing." In 2004, *Potentials* magazine gave an estimate of $21 billion a year for the market in all "motivational products" (Steven Winn, "Overcome That Gnawing Fear of Success," *San Francisco Chronicle*, May 24, 2004). The International Coach Federation estimates that coaches worldwide garnered $1.5 billion in 2007 and that most of them were business coaches (Executive Summary, ICF Global Coaching Study, revised Feb. 2008).

Albertsons, Allstate, Caterpillar, Exxon Mobil, and American Airlines among the corporate clients.[3] And companies can command the attention of their employees, requiring them to attend coaching sessions, listen to DVDs, or show up at motivational events. Many of the people who attend "Get Motivated!" events do so with free tickets provided by their employers.

In the hands of employers, positive thinking has been transformed into something its nineteenth-century proponents probably never imagined—not an exhortation to get up and get going but a means of social control in the workplace, a goad to perform at ever-higher levels. The publishers of Norman Vincent Peale's *Power of Positive Thinking* were among the first to see this potential way back in the fifties, urging, in an ad for that book: "EXECUTIVES: Give this book to employees. It pays dividends!" Salesmen would gain "renewed faith in what they sell and in their organization," plus, the ad promised, the book would bring "greater efficiency from the *office staff*. Marked reductions in clock-watching."[4] With "motivation" as the whip, positive thinking became the hallmark of the compliant employee, and as the conditions of corporate employment worsened in the age of downsizing that began in the 1980s, the hand on the whip grew heavier.

Lonely Salesmen

Salespeople didn't need any prompting from management to buy into positive thinking, and for understandable reasons. Theirs is a lonely existence, as Sue Goodhart told me, typically cut off from company headquarters and lived out in the perpetual exile of highways, motels, and airports. As much as anyone in the corporation, they face a life of constant challenge, in which every day is a test likely to end in rejection and defeat. But however lonely and wounded, the salesman has to be prepared to pick himself up and generate fresh enthusiasm for the next customer, the next city, the next rejection. He—and, as the twentieth century wore on, increasingly she—urgently needed a way to overcome self-doubts and generate optimism.

Consider the Internet testimony of a salesman named Rob Spiegel, who describes himself as initially skeptical of positive thinking: "My doubts centered on the thought that positive thinking wasn't much different than magical thinking. . . . Even more disturbing, I worried that positive thinking may be a nasty form of self delusion that could ultimately clothe you into an unreality that could actually prevent success." But once he started his own business—he does not say in what—he came to understand the need for a defensive reprogramming of his mind:

> When you roll up your sleeves and begin the heavy lifting of starting a company, doom thoughts quickly fill your empty brain. Every "NO" from a sales call is a powerful referendum on the very idea that you could successfully launch a business. If you're not thinking positively in the face of rejection, you eventually believe those who are rejecting you, and during the early stages, there's more rejection than acceptance.[5]

The centrality of the sales effort to the consumer economy cannot be underestimated: if that economy is to flourish, people have to be persuaded to buy things they do not need or do not know they need, and this persuasion is the job of the sales force as well as the advertising agencies. But for all their contributions to economic growth, salespeople get very little respect. In Woody Allen's film *Take the Money and Run*, Allen's character is tortured by being locked up in a room with an insurance salesman. We find salespeople's enthusiasm false; we think of them as the quintessentially hollowed-out men. The twentieth century saw two great plays about salesmen—Arthur Miller's *Death of a Salesman* and David Mamet's *Glengarry Glen Ross*—and in each of them the drama hinges on the fact that some flicker of humanity remains within the salesmen's shriveled souls.

It was to this despised group that Norman Vincent Peale took his ministry beginning in the 1950s. Although he enjoyed consorting with top business leaders, he especially liked speaking to the lowly salesmen, even to the point of seeing himself as one of them—"God's salesman," as he liked to say. Surely, except for the constant rejection, his life resembled those of the salesmen to whom he preached positive thinking. After the success of *The Power of Positive Thinking*, Peale never ceased traveling and speaking, leaving his children to be raised by his wife and his church to be tended by his staff, so that he shared with salesmen their "nomadic, endlessly mobile, existences, aware that every transaction was an individual performance and a personal challenge," as a biographer puts it.[6] In *The Power of Positive Thinking*, most of his anecdotes are set in hotels or conference rooms, where anxious or shattered salesmen buttonhole him for personal counseling. This was Peale's designated constituency—"the lonely man in the motel room."[7]

Today salespeople are hardly alone in their efforts to achieve a state of frenzied enthusiasm; they get plenty of help from their employers, who have become increasingly ingenious in their motivational efforts. One approach, pioneered by the pharmaceutical companies, is to start by hiring people who are already, in a sense, motivators themselves—college cheerleaders—and they have turned out to be so successful as sales reps that a regular recruiting pipeline has developed between the drug companies and the campuses. "They don't ask what the major is," a cheerleading adviser at the University of Kentucky said of the recruiters; it's enough for the job candidate to be a trained cheerleader. "Exaggerated motions, exaggerated smiles, exaggerated enthusiasm," the adviser continued, "they learn those things, and they can get people to do what they want."[8] Another straightforward way to motivate a sales force is to offer rewards for high performers. Top sellers of Mary Kay cosmetics get pink Cadillacs; the "employee of the month" at any company may get a more convenient parking space. A management consultant observed in 2006 that "U.S. employers spend $100 billion a year on incentives like T-shirts, golf outings and free trips to Florida in the belief that they somehow motivate and inspire their employees."[9]

Not all the motivational methods applied to salespeople feature rewards and incentives. In a workplace environment where employees have few if any rights, some companies resort to motivating their salespeople in ways that are cruel or even kinky. Alarm One, for example, a California-based home-security company, was sued in 2006 by a saleswoman for subjecting her to what could be called motivational spankings. The spankings, usually administered with the metal yard signs of competing companies, were meant to spur competition between teams of salespersons. As one salesman testified, "Basically, you'd get up in front of the room, put your hands on the wall, bend over, and get hit with the sign." Other punishments for underperforming salespersons included having eggs broken on their heads or whipped cream sprayed on their faces and being forced to wear diapers. (Since both men and women were subjected to them, the spankings did not qualify as sexual harassment, and the woman lost her suit.)

An even more disturbing case comes from Prosper Inc. in Provo, Utah, where in May 2007 a supervisor subjected an employee to waterboarding as part of a "motivational exercise." The employee, who had volunteered for the experience without knowing what was involved, was taken outside, told to lie down with his head pointed downhill, and held in place by fellow employees while the supervisor poured water into his nose and mouth. "You saw how hard Chad fought for air right there," the supervisor reportedly told the sales team. "I want you to go back inside and fight that hard to make sales."[10] While insisting that the company does not condone torture, Prosper management has had nothing to say about this supervisor's more routine motivational practices, like drawing mustaches on employees' faces and making them work standing up all day. Oddly enough, Prosper is itself in the business of selling "motivation" to other companies.

Far more commonly, of course, companies have left their salespeople's bodies untouched and sought only to control their minds. When sociologist Robin Leidner underwent sales training at a company called Combined Insurance in 1987, he found an "emphasis on teaching proper attitudes and selling techniques and [a] relative lack of attention to teaching agents about life insurance." The first day of class began with trainees standing up and chanting, "I FEEL HEALTHY, I FEEL HAPPY, I FEEL TERRIFIC!" while throwing "the winning punch." At Combined Insurance, this was part of the "Positive Mental Attitude" philosophy developed by the company's founder, W. Clement Stone—a major Republican donor and coauthor, with Napoleon Hill, of *Success through a Positive Mental Attitude*. Slogans flashed at sales trainees on video included "I dare you to develop a winning personality." Leidner comments, "As that last slogan makes clear, trainees were encouraged to regard their personalities as something to be worked on and adjusted to promote success."[11]

Few companies have worked as hard to instill positive thinking in their sales force as Amway, the purveyor of cleaning products, water purifiers, and cosmetics. Amway recruits undergo an intense indoctrination, paid for out of their own pockets, in the form of tapes, books, seminars, and rallies. In the early 1980s, salespeople were expected to buy a book a month from a list including such classics as *The Power of Positive Thinking* and Napoleon Hill's *Think and Grow Rich!*[12] At seminars, which the salespeople pay to attend, they learn that "God is Positive, and the Devil is Negative." As one former Amway salesman explains, "Whatever influence weakens your belief and commitment in the business is Negative. . . . Refusal to buy a tape when recommended by the upline [people higher in the sales hierarchy] is Negative." This salesman describes an Amway sales rally as something like a rock concert:

> Waves of reciprocal chanting sweep back and forth over the hall, one side shouting, "Ain't it Great!" and the other answering, "Ain't it Though!" In a regional event, thousands flick their Bics, or other brand-name propane lighters (Amway does not yet manufacture one) and whirl the flames in a circle to symbolize the mystical force of the [company's current sales] Plan. . . . Slogans and circles are flashed on a huge video screen at the front of the amphitheater, strobe-light style, in time to the music.[13]

Not to throw oneself wholeheartedly into the frenzy would, of course, be "Negative."

As anyone who's attended a sports event, a revival meeting, or a real rock concert knows, it's hard to resist the excitement of a crowd. When the music's pounding and others are standing, chanting, or swaying, we are involuntarily drawn in and may briefly experience a sense of exaltation, of being part of "something larger than ourselves." Motivational speakers—and event planners—understand and exploit this human capacity, often demanding that the audience stand and perhaps chant or dance in place. In his book on the motivational-speaking business, Jonathan Black describes one speaker's audiences as "*transformed employees*," who occasionally "break down in sobs." After the performance, "they clasp [the speaker's] hands and tell him he's their savior. They hug him, shaking and crying."[14] For an anxious salesperson or cubicle dweller, an event like this can be a thrillingly cathartic experience—not something to resent, as an attempt at mind control, but something to expect at any company gathering and even feel entitled to as a temporary release from the ongoing pressure.

By the start of the twenty-first century, canned motivation had ceased to be a sideshow to the main drama of the corporate world and begun to penetrate to the heart of American business. Not only salespeople but other white-collar workers, IT people, engineers, and accountants are now increasingly found to be in need of motivation and its promised results—positive thinking and improved performance. Everyone in the corporate world, it seems, is in danger of falling into a nonproductive funk unless continually propped up by fresh doses of motivational adrenaline. And perhaps the most surprising converts to positive thinking are the actual decision makers—the executives and managers.

The Era of Irrationality

When I talk to relative insiders about the corporate market for motivation, they often seem uncomfortable with its loopier aspects—sales events that resemble political rallies or revival meetings, for example, and the promise of omnipotence through the law of attraction. James Champy, a management consultant and coauthor of the 1993 best seller *Reengineering the Corporation,* said he finds much of the motivational oeuvre "delusional" and its practitioners

often "cads." Clarke Caywood, a professor of marketing at North-
western, admitted to being too "over-educated and cynical" for
motivational tricks like visualization but insisted that they "can't
hurt": "If you learn just one little trick—like putting a picture of
the boat that you want on your mirror—that could be what leads
to a sale." He and I—a professor and a writer, respectively—might
realize that visualizing a boat will not bring it to you, but it would
be "arrogant," he told me, to deny that most corporate employees,
especially salespeople, need to rely on such "tricks" just to get them
through the day.

Corporate managers had thought of themselves, through much
of the twentieth century, as cool-headed professionals trained in
"management science" and performing a public service by making firms run smoothly and efficiently. Arising in the early part of
the century, at the same time that medicine and engineering were
organizing themselves into professions, professional management
reflected a widespread middle-class faith—antithetical to the tenets of positive thinking—that all problems would yield to a rational, scientific approach. Why bother with wishful thinking when
science and technology were already generating such fabulous in-
novations as the automobile, the telephone, and the radio? The
college-educated American middle class hewed to one central belief: that the goal was progress for all, not just individual success,
and that it would be achieved through the work of highly trained,
rational, dispassionate specialists.

There never was a body of management "science" in the way
that there is, for example, a body of medical science; there were
only case studies to ponder and what we now call "best practices"
to review. But the notion that management was a rational enterprise that anyone could master through study had a powerful
meritocratic thrust, challenging the old practice of replacing business leaders with their sons or sons-in-law. The number of people

employed as corporate managers ballooned in the postwar period; business became the most popular undergraduate major and the MBA the most popular graduate degree—all based on the idea that management was an impersonal, rational undertaking.

Then, in the 1980s, came the paroxysm of downsizing, and the very nature of the corporation was thrown into doubt. In what began almost as a fad and quickly matured into an unshakable habit, companies were "restructuring," "reengineering," and generally cutting as many jobs as possible, white collar as well as blue. Between 1980 and 1985, General Electric's CEO, Jack Welch, earned his nickname of "Neutron Jack" by laying off 112,000 employees and announcing his intention to eliminate the bottom-performing 10 percent every year. Soon shareholders throughout the corporate world were demanding constant "reductions in force" (RIFs) as a way of boosting share prices, at least in the short term. The *New York Times* captured the new corporate order succinctly in 1987, reporting that it "eschews loyalty to workers, products, corporate structures, businesses, factories, communities, even the nation. All such allegiances are viewed as expendable under the new rules. With survival at stake, only market leadership, strong profits and a high stock price can be allowed to matter."[15]

Corporations had once been task-oriented entities, created in the nineteenth century through charters to perform specific projects like canal or railroad building. The word "corporate" still suggests a group engaged in some collective undertaking—beyond making money for shareholders—and well into the postwar period corporations continued to define themselves in terms of their products and overall contribution to society. But with the advent of "finance capitalism" in the 1980s, shareholders' profits came to trump all other considerations, even pride in the product. Harvard Business School's Rakesh Khurana, who has chronicled the decline of professional management, traces the changing conception of the corporation through policy statements made by the Business Roundtable. In 1990, this body representing America's large corporations stated that "corporations are chartered to serve both their shareholders and society as a whole," including such stakeholders as employees, customers, suppliers, and communities. In 1997, however, the Roundtable explicitly denied any responsibility to stakeholders other than shareholders, stating that "the notion that the board must somehow balance the interests of other stakeholders fundamentally misconstrues the role of directors." Relieved of any concern for employees, customers, and "society as a whole," corporations degenerated into mere "aggregations of financial assets" to be plundered, disaggregated, or merged into one another at will. Some management thinkers even began to describe the corporation as "a legal fiction, a ghost of the mind," because the product was increasingly incidental and the bonds between corporate employees were increasingly fragile.[16] Business advice books like *Swim with the Sharks without Being Eaten Alive* stressed that in the new corporate setting it was every man for himself.

High-level managers came to realize that they were no less expendable than anyone else. A hostile takeover or a sudden decision to eliminate a product line or division could send them packing at any time; even CEOs were being churned in and out of their jobs. But the higher-ups had one great advantage over the average employee living under the threat of layoffs: because they were increasingly rewarded with stock options—and often with golden parachutes—they stood a chance of striking it rich in the ongoing turmoil.

The combination of great danger and potentially dazzling rewards makes for a potent cocktail—leading, in this case, to a wave of giddiness that swept through America's managerial class. Rejecting the old, slow, thoughtful methods of professional management,

American managers became enamored of intuition, snap judgments, and hunches. As business guru Tom Peters observed, "Things
are moving too fast for us to sort out logically what's going on."[17]
An article in *Fast Company* complained that "there's this one big
rub about management books—even the best-selling ones and
even the ones with plenty of data attached. The world they seek to
describe is so complex, so tumultuous, often so random as to defy
predictability and even rationality."[18] Or, as *BusinessWeek* put it
in 1999: "Who has time for decision trees and five-year plans anymore? Unlike the marketplace of 20 years ago, today's information and services-dominated economy is all about instantaneous
decision-making"—and that had to be based on gut feelings or
sudden, inexplicable revelations.[19] Hesitating or spending too long
on a decision was now condemned as "overanalyzing" or "overin-
tellectualizing." The only workable "paradigm" was change itself,
and the only way to survive was to embrace it wholeheartedly or,
in Peters's words, learn to "thrive on chaos."

At the top of the managerial hierarchy, CEOs forged a new
self-image as charismatic leaders who could be counted on to
have the right intuitions and gut feelings in a fast-changing world.
The old-style CEO had risen from within the ranks of the company, mastering every aspect of the business before ascending to
the top; the new one was likely to have been hired for his celebrity
status in the business world, even if it was derived from totally
unrelated lines of businesses. As Khurana describes the transformation: "The image of a CEO changed from being a capable ad-
ministrator to a *leader*—a motivating, flamboyant leader"—very
much like a motivational speaker, in fact.[20] Some business school
academics found a disturbing element of the divine in the new
CEO self-image. According to a 2002 article in the journal *Human Relations*, many business leaders "develop a monomaniacal
conviction that there is one right way of doing things, and believe

they possess an almost divine insight into reality." They were now convinced, in no small part by the motivational gurus who were replacing the old management "consultants," that "they are charismatic visionaries rather than people in suits."[21]

Forsaking the "science" of management, corporate leaders began a wild thrashing around in search of new ways to explain an increasingly uncertain world—everything from chaos theory to Native American wisdom, from "excellence" to Eastern religions. It wasn't enough to reject the old approaches; a kind of antirationality gripped American business. With a nod to management's past commitment to rational analysis, *BusinessWeek* admitted that "spiritual thinking in Corporate America may seem as out of place as a typewriter at a high-tech company." But as the cover story went on to report, it was everywhere. A 1999 gathering, for example, of "some of the world's youngest and most powerful chief executives" featured a "shamanic healing journey":

> There, in a candlelit room thick with a haze of incense, 17 blindfolded captains of industry lay on towels, breathed deeply, and delved into the "lower world" to the sound of a lone tribal drum. Leading the group was Richard Whiteley, a Harvard business school–educated best-selling author and management consultant who moonlights as an urban shaman. "Envision an entrance into the earth, a well, or a swimming hole," Whiteley half-whispered above the sea of heaving chests. He then instructed the executives how to retrieve from their inner depths their "power animals, who would guide their companies to 21st century success."[22]

Not only shamanic healing but dozens of forms of spiritual practice proliferated within corporate American in the 1990s and

2000s. There were "vision quests" and Native American healing circles for top managers, as well as prayer groups, Buddhist seminars, fire walking, exercises in "tribal story telling" and "deep listening." At the beginning of the 1990s, Esalen, the Big Sur spa that had been a bastion of the counterculture in the 1960s and 1970s, was raising money to turn its main building into a luxurious corporate retreat, and major companies like AT&T, DuPont, TRW, Ford, and Proctor and Gamble were buying up spiritual experiences for their higher-level managers. "Corporations are full of mystics," a 1996 business self-help book declared. "If you want to find a genuine mystic, you are more likely to find one in a boardroom than in a monastery or cathedral."[23]

In the newly "spiritual" corporate culture, there was nothing at all unsettling about positive thinking and its promise that the law of attraction allows you to control the world with your thoughts. As *Fortune* observed, the new business spirituality offered "a world view in which . . . reality is not absolute but a by-product of human consciousness."[24] Traditional number-crunching management consultants began to give way to self-described management gurus like Peters and Tony Robbins—best-selling celebrities who could bring an audience to their feet with spirited renditions of the old positive-thinking nostrums.

The decline of management as a rational undertaking can be traced through the meteoric career of Peters, dubbed the "uberguru" of management by the *Los Angeles Times*. He started as an analyst at the old-line, hyperrational McKinsey consulting firm, only to discover the "human element" in management in his 1982 best seller, *In Search of Excellence*. It was not enough to manage "by the numbers," he and his coauthor argued, reasonably enough. Employees need to be motivated and rewarded for going the extra mile to satisfy customers, and this involved engaging their emotions. Corporations were made up of people, people are emotional beings, so management would just have to wade into this murky new territory. Peters, in other words, made a rational case for a new, less-than-rational approach to management based on motivation, mood boosting, and positive thinking.

But as the age of downsizing wore on, a menacingly nihilistic tone crept into his message. It was no longer enough to "thrive on chaos," as his 1988 book advised—the forward-looking manager should actually generate it. "Destroy your corporation before a competitor does!" he wrote in his 1992 book, *Liberation Management.* "Disorganize! And keep disorganizing!"[25] He issued no statement without his trademark red exclamation marks; he posed for photos in his boxer shorts. A 2000 article on Peters in *Fortune* began: "If you know one thing about Tom Peters, you know about his first book, and if you know two things, the second is that he hasn't written a book as good as that since, and if you know three things, the third is that sometime in the 18 years since that first precious book, he's gone bonkers."[26]

Maybe it was the boxer shorts and Peters's increasingly madcap speaking style that turned *Fortune* against him, because, no matter how bonkers, he had not in fact lost touch with corporate America. *Downsize* was his message for the 1990s—destroy the corporation as we know it—and this is exactly what the CEOs did. When Jack Welch retired from his chairmanship of GE in 2001, he ended his good-bye speech on a note every bit as nihilistic as Peters's message, "by telling everyone to turn the organization upside down, shake it up, and go blow the roof off."[27] Did layoffs strengthen or weaken the corporation? A mid-1990s study by the American Management Association found no positive impact on productivity.[28] But it hardly mattered, since layoffs clearly led to increased share prices, at least in the short term. If there was a deity at the center of corporate America's new "business spirituality," it was Shiva, the dancing god of destruction.

Managing Despair

Between 1981 and 2003, about thirty million full-time American workers lost their jobs in corporate downsizings.[29] American institutions—corporate and governmental—had little of concrete value to offer the victims of this massive social dislocation. Unemployment benefits generally run out after six months; health insurance ceases with employment. Many of the downsized white-collar workers bounced back, finding new jobs—although paying an average of 17 percent less than their former salaries—or adjusting to life as contract workers or "consultants" of one sort or another.[30] But without a safety net, formerly middle-class people often tumbled quickly into low-wage jobs and even destitution. I have met, and heard from, many of these downwardly mobile former managers and professionals: the IT marketing woman in Atlanta who worked six months as a janitor between marketing jobs; the Minneapolis car service driver who gives his passengers his old business card, from when he was a media executive, in case they might be interested in hiring one; the chemical engineer whose layoff resulted in a stint in homeless shelters. The once stable middle class of white-collar workers, who had been brought up to believe that their skills and education would guarantee security, was reduced to anxious scrambling.

Downsizing did not, of course, increase the number of salespeople, but it did increase the number of people who were encouraged to *think* of themselves as salespeople. In the hazardous new corporate workplace, everyone was encouraged to engage in a continual sales effort, selling him- or herself. As anthropologist Charles N. Darrah put it, the white-collar worker had become a "bundle of skills . . . who can move freely between [workplace] settings, carrying his or her skills like so much luggage."[31] But he or she could hope to move "freely" only by constantly working on and burnishing what Tom Peters termed "the brand called you." No longer were you to think of yourself as an "employee"; you were "a brand that shouts distinction, commitment, and passion!"[32] Everyone, from software writer to accountant, was now subject to the same insecurities as the "lonely salesman" once targeted by Norman Vincent Peale.

The motivation industry could not repair this new reality. All it could do was offer to change how one *thought* about it, insisting that corporate restructuring was an exhilaratingly progressive "change" to be embraced, that job loss presented an opportunity for self-transformation, that a new batch of "winners" would emerge from the turmoil. And this is what corporations were paying the motivation industry to do. As the *Washington Post* reported in a 1994 article on motivational products, "Large corporations are looking for innovative and cheap ways to boost employees demoralized by massive layoffs."[33] According to a "history of coaching" on the Internet, the coaching industry owed its huge growth in the 1990s to "the loss of 'careers for life.'"[34] AT&T sent its San Francisco staff to a big-tent motivational event called "Success 1994" on the same day the company announced that it would lay off fifteen thousand workers in the coming two years. As *Time*'s Richard Reeves reported, the message of the featured speaker—the frenetic Christian motivator Zig Ziglar—was, "It's your own fault; don't blame the system; don't blame the boss—work harder and pray more."[35]

Products like motivational posters and calendars also owed their market to what a Successories spokeswoman described, in a tactfully abstract fashion, as "a lot of negativity in the world." "We need [Successories products] because there's a lot of companies downsizing and companies that can't afford to give their employees the raises they were expecting," she said, and her company's offerings are "one of the ways to smooth that over."[36] As Ralph

Whitehead, a University of Massachusetts at Amherst professor of journalism, observed, "Corporate downsizers fire every third person and then put up inspirational posters in the halls to cover the psychic wounds."[37]

Think of it as a massive experiment in mind control. "Reality sucks," a computer scientist with a master's degree who can find only short-term, benefit-free contract jobs told me. But you can't change reality, at least not in any easy and obvious way. You could join a social movement working to create an adequate safety net or to bring about more humane corporate policies, but those efforts might take a lifetime. For now, you can only change your perception of reality, from negative and bitter to positive and accepting. This was the corporate world's great gift to its laid-off employees and the overworked survivors—positive thinking.

Companies brought in motivational speakers for an ever-growing number of corporate meetings.[38] Whatever else goes on at these meetings—the presentation of awards, the introduction of new executives—the "entertainment" is usually provided by motivational speakers. As Vicki Sullivan, who follows the market for such speakers, said at the National Speakers Association conference in 2007, corporations are the "sugar daddies" of the motivational speaking industry. "At some point," she told me in an interview, employers realized it was not enough to expose people to familiar positive-thinking nostrums like "Don't read newspapers or talk to negative people." Instead, she said, "What they've learned is that you have to go beyond that, as change happens faster and faster. You have to use motivational speakers to help people hang in there."

Motivational speakers and coaches promoted themselves as a tool for managing "change," meaning layoffs and the extra workload imposed on layoff survivors. A coaching company, for example, promised to cure the toxic atmosphere left by downsizing:

"This program is perfect for organizations and corporations that are going through change such as downsizing, mergers or acquisitions. If the people in your organization are reacting with resistance to change, coffee room gossip, decreased performance, declining communication, or increased stress, this change management training teaches how to stay positively motivated and focused."[39] One unusually forthcoming motivational speaker expressed some discomfort with her role, telling me that employers use people like her in part "to beat up employees" if they don't achieve the goals that have been set for them. "They can say, 'Didn't you listen to the speaker we brought in?'"

The burgeoning genre of business self-help books provided another way to get white-collar workers to adapt to downsizing. Of these, the classic of downsizing propaganda was *Who Moved My Cheese?*, which has sold ten million copies, in no small part due to companies that bought it in bulk for their employees. Perhaps in recognition of the fact that it would fall into the hands of many reluctant readers, it's a tiny volume, only ninety-four pages of large print, offering the kind of fable appropriate to a children's book. Two little maze-dwelling, cheese-eating people named Hem and Haw—for the human tendency to think and reflect—arrive at their "Cheese Station" one day to find that the cheese is gone. The "Littlepeople" waste time ranting and raving "at the injustice of it all," as the book's title suggests. But there are also two mice in the maze, who scurry off without hesitation to locate an alternative cheese source, because, being rodents, they "kept life simple. They didn't overanalyze or overcomplicate things."[40]

Finally the little humans learn from the mice that they may have to adapt to a *new* cheese. Haw uses what amounts to the law of attraction to find it: he starts to "paint a picture in his mind . . . in great realistic detail, [of himself] sitting in the middle of a pile of all his favorite cheeses—from Cheddar to Brie!"[41] Instead of resenting the loss of his old cheese, he realizes, more positively, that "change could lead to something better" and is soon snacking on a "delicious" new cheese. Lesson for victims of layoffs: the dangerous human tendencies to "overanalyze" and complain must be overcome for a more rodentlike approach to life. When you lose a job, just shut up and scamper along to the next one.

Companies employed a variety of positive-sounding euphemisms for layoffs, describing them as "releases of resources" or "career-change opportunities," but the actual process was swift and brutal.[42] By the 1990s, managing the actual layoffs had become a specialized art in itself, often practiced by restructuring experts brought in from outside. For one thing, the layoffs had to be announced suddenly and all at once, so there would be no time for the grumblings of the victims to infect the surviving workforce. Typically it was the company's security force that managed the actual people-removing process and ensured that the discarded workers left without making a fuss. In the usual scenario, a person would be told of his or her layoff and quickly escorted by a security guard to the door. Sometimes discarded employees would be given a chance to pack up any personal effects they had in their offices—family photographs, for example—and sometimes these things would just be shipped to them later.

To limit ill will, if only to head off wrongful-termination suits and bad-mouthing by former employees, employers turned to outplacement firms, which, in addition to training in résumé writing, offered to console the laid-off with motivational services. The owner of an outplacement company in Portland, Oregon, asserted in 1994 that, with his help, people came to see "that losing a job was a step forward in their lives, . . . a growth experience, self-retreat, a needed time out." The *Los Angeles Times* reported on the case of Primalde Lodhia, an Indian-born MBA, computer scientist, and mechanical engineer who was laid off in 1991 with no explanation other than "We are very happy with your work, but we have to let you go. You don't fit in our management." The company offered him outplacement services; he asked for cash instead, but the company insisted. In the motivational halfway house of outplacement, Lodhia was advised not to talk to anyone about his job loss for a month. He complied, later telling the *Times*, "It was good advice. I was so bitter, I would have said things that would have been bad for me."[43]

Not all companies rely on outplacement firms, which often charge over $10,000 per layoff victim, instead expecting their discarded employees to seek out and pay for their own motivational services. I attended about a dozen of these networking events and "boot camps" for white-collar job seekers in 2005 and found that the core message was positive thinking: whatever happens to you is a result of your attitude; by overcoming bitterness and converting to a positive or "winning" attitude, you could attract the job of your dreams. In her research on laid-off tech workers in the early 2000s, Carrie Lane, a professor of American studies, found the same thing. Events targeting laid-off workers "subtly urged [them] to snap out of it and start acting like a good (optimistic and industrious) jobseeker."[44]

After the layoff victims had been winnowed out and perhaps further isolated, like Lodhia, with advice not to communicate with others, there were the shocked and anxious survivors to deal with, and here again management turned to the motivation industry. Business journalist Jill Andresky Fraser calls the motivational effort "internal public relations," used to create "pumped-up, motivated converts who would be ready to thrive under the most grueling and even hostile of business conditions." For example, in the midst of downsizing in the mid-1990s, NYNEX subjected its employees to mandatory exercises, such as one in which you had to show how many ways you could jump around a room: "So [the employees] jumped—on one leg, on both legs, with their hands in the air, with one hand covering an eye. They jumped and they jumped and they jumped some more. . . . Then the leaders would say things like, " 'Look at how creative you are, how many different ways you can manage to jump around the room.' "[45]

But the most popular technique for motivating the survivors of downsizing was "team building"—an effort so massive that it has spawned a "team-building industry" overlapping the motivation industry. Just as layoffs were making a mockery of the team concept, employees were urged to find camaraderie and a sense of collective purpose at the microlevel of the "team." And the less teamlike the overall organization became with the threat of continued downsizing, the more management insisted on individual devotion to these largely fictional units. "Rather than eliminate or postpone teams, organizations should consider the benefits teams can offer in a downsizing phase," a management consultant and "organizational change" expert wrote. "The team system offers a form of camaraderie that helps promote teamwork around getting the job done and enables people to feel connected to something smaller and safer than a large organization. People generally have an innate need to feel connected to a small group of people. . . . Teams offer this in the work environment."[46]

In search of team spirit, team-building companies offered dozens of "fun" bonding exercises, indoor and outdoor—simple ones involving balloons, blindfolds, or buckets of water and more intensive ones such as weeklong wilderness excursions. The idea was to whip up a fervent devotion to the firm even as it threatened to eliminate you. As a downsized AT&T worker told the *PBS Evening News Hour* in 1996: "We went to Outward Bound, the phone center people, for a week, and you bonded with everybody in the country. It was the most incredible thing I've ever been through. You were a family. You were the most dedicated people in the world. I mean, if your kids didn't stand up and do the Pledge of Allegiance to an AT&T commercial, you know—"[47]

Team building is, in other words, another form of motivation, with the difference being that, in the desolate environment of the downsized corporation, this motivation was supposed to be generated from within the work group or "team." One group offering both motivational and team-building services makes this clear on its Web site—though not too clear, given the garbled English that is another characteristic of the postrational corporate world: "In this team building workshop, you will learn both the team building skills and motivation skills guaranteed to make your team more cohesive, increase employee morale, and motivated. You'll learn how to build a team that grumbles less and works more, discipline less and reward more, create more focused and productive meetings and get recognized by the organization."[48]

As for the connection to old-fashioned, Peale-style positive thinking, the literature and coaches emphasize that a good "team player" is by definition a "positive person." He or she smiles frequently, does not complain, is not overly critical, and gracefully submits to whatever the boss demands.

Sometimes the motivational effort backfired, especially when combined with ongoing layoffs. In the mid-1990s, while shedding 20 percent of its workforce, NYNEX initiated a "Winning Ways" program aimed at instilling employees with "the mentality of a winner," but the employees sneeringly relabeled it "Whining Ways."[49] When E. L. Kersten was working for a Dallas Internet service provider, he took note of the motivational products the company president favored and got the brilliant idea of going into business selling parodies of them. One of the "demotivational" posters available at Kersten's despair.com site shows a bear about to snap up a salmon swimming upstream. The caption reads: "The journey of a thousand miles sometimes ends very, very badly." Another one shows a beautiful shoreline at sunset, with the caption "If a pretty poster and a cute saying are all it takes to motivate you, you probably have a very easy job. The kind robots will be doing soon."

But such creative cynicism was rare. By and large, America's white-collar corporate workforce drank the Kool-Aid, as the expression goes, and accepted positive thinking as a substitute for their former affluence and security. They did not take to the streets, shift their political allegiance in large numbers, or show up at work with automatic weapons in hand. As one laid-off executive told me with quiet pride, "I've gotten over my negative feelings, which were so dysfunctional." Positive thinking promised them a sense of control in a world where the "cheese" was always moving. They may have had less and less power to chart their own futures, but they had been given a worldview—a belief system, almost a religion—that claimed they were in fact infinitely powerful, if only they could master their own minds.

FIVE

God Wants You
to Be Rich

The most eye-catching religious development of the late twentieth century was the revival of fire-and-brimstone Calvinism known as the Christian right. But while its foremost representatives, televangelists Jerry Falwell and Pat Robertson, hurled denunciations at "sinners" like gays and feminists and predicted the imminent end of the world, a friendlier approach was steadily gaining ground— positive thinking, disguised now as Christianity. Calvinism and positive thinking had last squared off in the nineteenth century, when positive thinking was still known as New Thought, and they did so again near the turn of the twenty-first century, not in public clashes but in a quiet fight for market share—television audiences, book sales, and ever-growing congregations. Promulgated from the pulpit, the message of positive thinking reached white-collar suburbanites who had so far encountered it only at work, as well as millions of low-wage and blue-collar people who had not yet encountered it at all.

By any quantitative measure, the most successful preachers today are the positive thinkers, who no longer mention sin and usually have little to say about those standard whipping boys of the Christian right, abortion and homosexuality. Gone is the threat of hell and the promise of salvation, along with the grim story of Jesus's torment on the cross; in fact, the cross has been all but banished from the largest and most popular temples of the new evangelism, the megachurches. Between 2001 and 2006, the number of megachurches—defined as having a weekly attendance of two thousand or more—doubled to 1,210, giving them a combined congregation of nearly 4.4 million.[1]

Instead of harsh judgments and harrowing tales of suffering and redemption, the new positive theology offered at megachurches (and many smaller churches) offers promises of wealth, success, and health in this life now, or at least very soon. You *can* have that new car or house or necklace, because God wants to "prosper you." In a 2006 *Time* poll, 17 percent of all American Christians, of whatever denomination or church size, said they consider themselves to be part of a "prosperity gospel" movement and a full 61 percent agreed with the statement that "God wants people to be prosperous."[2] How do you get prosperity to "manifest" in your life? Not through the ancient technique of prayer but through positive thinking. As one reporter observes of the megachurch message:

> Often resembling motivational speeches, the sermons
> are generally about how to live a successful life—or,
> "Jesus meets the power of positive thinking." They are
> encouraging, upbeat and usually follow on the heels
> of a music and video presentation. (After this, the last
> thing those in attendance want to hear is a sermon
> about "doom and gloom.") One will often hear phrases

such as "Keep a good attitude," "Don't get negative or bitter," "Be determined" and "Shake it off and step up."[3]

Televangelist Joyce Meyer writes that "I believe that more than any other thing, our attitude is what determines the kind of life we are going to have"—not our piety or faith but our *attitude*. "It's especially important to maintain a positive attitude," she explains on her Web site, "because God is positive."

Like many other proponents of the new theology, Meyer has good reason to be "positive." Her ministries—which extend to weight loss and self-esteem—have made her the centimillionaire owner of a private jet and a $23,000 antique marble toilet. So egregious is the wealth of top positive-thinking evangelists—much of it, of course, tax-deductible—that in 2007 Senator Chuck Grassley (R-IA) launched an investigation, not only of Meyer but of televangelists Creflo Dollar, Benny Hinn, and Kenneth and Gloria Copeland. If these pastors have been incautious about displaying their wealth, it's because, like secular motivational speakers, they hold themselves up as role models for success. Follow me, is the message—send money, tithe to my church, employ the methods outlined in my books—and you will become like me.

Joel Osteen of Houston's Lakewood Church is hardly a high roller among the positive evangelists. He flies in commercial planes and owns only one home, but he has been dubbed the "rock star" of the new gospel and called "America's most influential Christian" by the *Church Report* magazine.[4] Unlike many others who make their money by motivating people, Osteen has no history of painful obstacles overcome through sheer grit and determination. He inherited his church from his father, assuming the pulpit with no theological training after dropping out of Oral Roberts University. Once ensconced, he "grew" the church at a furious rate, till today it boasts a weekly attendance of forty thousand people and a weekly income of a million dollars. Osteen doesn't collect a salary from his church—there are already three hundred people on its payroll—because he is apparently content to live off his royalties. His first book, *Your Best Life Now*, has sold about four million copies, leading to what was said to be an advance of $13 million for the sequel, *Become a Better You*.

Osteen's books are easy to read, too easy—like wallowing in marshmallows. There is no argument, no narrative arc, just one anecdote following another, starring Osteen and his family members, various biblical figures, and a host of people identified by first name only. A criticism directed at Norman Vincent Peale in the 1950s applies just as well to Osteen's oeuvre: "The chapters of his books could easily be transposed from the beginning to the middle, or from the end to the beginning, or from one book to another. The paragraphs could be shuffled and rearranged in any order."[5] One of the best of Osteen's anecdotes involves a man who goes on a cruise ship carrying a suitcase full of crackers and cheese because he doesn't realize that meals are included with the price of his ticket. In other words, there's plenty for everyone—wealth, delightful buffet meals—if only we are prepared to demonstrate our faith by tithing generously to the church. His worst anecdotes, however, make the eyes glaze over, if not actually close, like the one that begins: "Growing up, my family had a dog named Scooter. He was a great big German shepherd, and he was the king of the neighborhood. Scooter was strong and fast, always chasing squirrels here and there, always on the go. Everybody knew not to mess with Scooter. One day my dad was out riding his bicycle. . . ."[6]

How to achieve the success, health, and happiness God wants you to have? Osteen's proffered technique is lifted directly from the secular positive thinkers—visualization. Other positive evangelists often emphasize the spoken word as well, and the need to speak your dream into existence through "positive confessions of faith and victory over your life." As Kenneth Hagin, one of the first positive preachers and a role model for Osteen, puts it: "Instead of speaking according to natural circumstances out of your head, learn to speak God's Word from your spirit. Begin to confess God's promises of life and health and victory into your situation. Then you can begin to enjoy God's abundant life as you have what you say!"[7] For Osteen and Hagin, as for Napoleon Hill and Norman Vincent Peale before them, success comes mainly through "reprogramming" your mind into positive mental images, based on what amounts to the law of attraction: "You will produce what you're continually seeing in your mind," Osteen promises. "Almost like a magnet," he writes, echoing Hill, "we draw in what we constantly think about." As evidence, Osteen offers many small "victories" in his life, like getting out of a speeding ticket and finding a parking space—not just any space, but "the premier spot in that parking lot." He suggests that the technique will also work "in a crowded restaurant": "You can say, 'Father, I thank you that I have favor with this hostess, and she's going to seat me soon.'"[8]

But Osteen's universe is not entirely tension-free. Within his world of easy wish fulfillment an "enemy" lurks, and it is negative thinking: "The enemy says you're not able to succeed; God says you can do all things through Christ. . . . The enemy says you'll never amount to anything; God says He will raise you up and make your life significant. The enemy says your problems are too big, there's no hope; God says He will solve those problems."[9] Robert Schuller, another leading positive pastor, invokes the same "enemy," advising his readers to *never verbalize a negative emotion* because to do so would mean "giving in and surrendering your will to an enemy."[10] Neither of these preachers personifies the "enemy" as Satan or condemns negative thinking as a sin; in fact, they never refer to either Satan or sin. But the old Calvinist Manichaeism persists in their otherwise sunny outlook: on the one side is goodness, godliness, and light; on the other is darkness and . . . doubt.

The God of Victory

There is nothing to mark Osteen's Lakewood Church, which I visited in the summer of 2008, as sanctified territory—no crosses, no stained glass windows, no images of Jesus. From my hotel room window, just across a six-lane highway from the church, it's a squat, warehouselike structure completely at home among the high-rise office buildings surrounding it. In fact, it used to be the Compaq Center, home stadium of the Houston Rockets, until Osteen acquired it in 1999 and transformed the interior into a 16,000-seat megachurch. Entering through an underground parking lot, I arrive in a cheery child-care area decorated with cartoon figures and lacking only popcorn to complete the resemblance to a suburban multiplex theater. Even the sanctuary, the former basketball court, carries on in this godless way. Instead of an altar, there is a stage featuring a rotating globe and flanked by artificial rocks enlivened with streams or what appears, at least, to be flowing water. I can find nothing suggestive of Christianity until I ascend to the second-floor bookstore—a sort of denatured and heavily censored version of Barnes and Noble, prominently displaying Joel Osteen's works, along with scores of products like scented candles and dinnerware embossed with scriptural quotes. Here, at last, are the crosses—large ones for wall hangings and discreet ones on vases, key chains, and mugs or stitched into ties and argyll socks.

The Osteens—Joel and his copastor and wife, Victoria—when they step forth on the stage for Sunday service to a standing ovation, are an attractive couple in their forties, but Joel is not quite the "walking advertisement for the success creed" I had read him described as.[11] He is shorter than she is, although on his book cover he appears at least two inches taller; his suit seems too large; and, what is also not evident in the book jacket photos, his curly, heavily gelled black hair has been styled into a definite mullet. She wears a ruffled white blouse with a black vest and slacks that do not quite mesh together at the waist, leaving a distracting white gap. In one way, the two of them seem perfectly matched, or at least symmetrical: his mouth is locked into the inverted triangle of his trademark smile, while her heavy dark brows stamp her face with angry tension, even when the mouth is smiling.

The production values are more sophisticated than the pastors themselves. Live music, extremely loud Christian rock devoid of any remotely African-derived beat, alternates with short bursts of speech in a carefully choreographed pattern. Joel, Victoria, or a senior pastor speaks for three to five minutes—their faces hugely amplified on the three large video screens above and to the sides of the stage—perhaps ending with a verbal segue into the next song, then stepping back as the chorus and lead singers move to center stage. All the while lights on the ceiling change color, dim and brighten, and occasionally flash, strobelike, to the beat. It's not stand-up-and-boogie music, but most of the congregation at least stands, sways, and raises an arm or two during the musical interludes, perhaps hoping to catch a glimpse of themselves on the video screens as the cameras pan the audience. "Disney," mutters the friend who has accompanied me, the wife of a local Baptist minister. But this is just a taping, and the twelve thousand or so of us in the sanctuary (the seats do not fill at either Sunday morning service) are only a studio audience. The real show, an edited version of what we are watching, will reach about seven million television viewers.

Inadvertently, I have come on a Sunday of immense importance to the Osteens, one of the greatest turning points, they aver,
in their lives. In the preceding week, a court had dismissed charges
against Victoria for assaulting and injuring a flight attendant.
The incident occurred in 2005, when they boarded the first-class
cabin of a flight bound for Vail, the ski resort, only to leave—or be
thrown off—the plane after Victoria raised a fuss over a small
"stain" or "spill" on the armrest of her seat. She demanded that the
flight attendant remove the stain immediately, and when the flight
attendant refused because she was busy helping other passengers
board, Victoria insisted, allegedly attempting to enter the cockpit
and complain to the pilots. Victoria ended up paying a $3,000 fine
imposed by the FAA, and the matter would have ended there if
the recalcitrant flight attendant had not brought suit demanding
10 percent of Victoria Osteen's net worth in compensation for al-
leged injuries, including hemorrhoids and a "loss of faith" due to
her mistreatment by a leading evangelist.

My friend's husband, the Baptist minister, had predicted when
we had coffee on Saturday that the Osteens' Sunday service would
make no mention of the whole ugly business. Why would they want
to revive the image of Victoria behaving, as another attendant on
the plane had testified, like a "combative diva"? He was wrong.
Both Sunday services are given over to Victoria's "victory" in court.
When Joel steps forth at the beginning of the service, he covers his
face with his hands, peekaboo fashion, for several seconds, and
when he removes them his eyes are red and his smile is in temporary remission. He then takes a large white handkerchief from his
pocket and rubs his eyes vigorously, although no tears are visible
on his magnified video image. "It's not just a victory for us," he
announces. "It's a victory for God's kingdom," hence the entire
service will be a "celebration." As the service proceeds, he tells us
that he spent his time at the trial writing out scriptural quotes

and shows us the yellow legal pad he used. He shares a long, muddled anecdote about how he had ended up wearing the suit he intended to testify in although he hadn't known he was going to testify on that particular day, because he couldn't "find another suit," leaving us to think that he owns no more than two. More ominously, he tells us that God "is against those who are against us."

When Victoria takes center stage, she's as triumphant as David doing his victory dance through the streets of Jerusalem, even briefly jumping up and down in joy. The "situation," as she calls it, was difficult and humiliating, but "I placed a banner of victory over my head"—figuratively, I assume, and not as an actual scarf. Oddly, there are no lessons learned, no humility acquired through adversity, not even any conventional expressions of gratitude to her husband for standing by her. This seems shabby even by the standards of that other positive preacher Robert Schuller of Orange County's megachurch, the Crystal Cathedral. When he had a similar altercation with a first-class flight attendant in 1997—such are the hazards of commercial air travel when you are accustomed to having your own servants—he ended up apologizing in court. But for Victoria, the only takeaways are that "we can't be bogged down by circumstances" and "don't lick your wounds," which echo Joel's constant exhortations to be "a victor, not a victim." In fact, sometime in the interval since the incident, God had revealed that he wanted her to write a book, and—good news!—it will be coming out in October, followed by a children's book a few months later.

I look around cautiously to see how everyone else is reacting to this celebration of a millionaire's court victory over a working woman, who happened in this case to be African American. The crowd, which is about two-thirds black and Latino and appears to contain few people who have ever landed a lucrative book contract

or flown first-class, applauds Victoria enthusiastically, many raising their arms, palms up, to the deity who engineered her triumph.
Maybe they hadn't followed the case or maybe they are just trying
to snatch a little of Victoria's victory for themselves, because the
message to this largely working-class congregation seems to be
that they, too, will triumph, as Victoria has, because that is God's
promise to them. It just may take a little time, because theirs seems
to be a forgetful God, who has to be "reminded" of his promises,
Joel told us. "Remember your promises," one of the songs goes, "remember your people, remember your children," as if addressing a
deadbeat dad. Focus on what you want, in other words, and eventually, after many importunings, God will give it to you.

There are traces of the old Christianity at Lakewood Church—
or perhaps I should say traces of religion in general—lingering
like the echoes of archaic chthonic cults that could still be found
in classical Greek mythology and ritual. "God" makes many ap-
pearances, often as "God in Christ Jesus," and Victoria refers often to anointings with oil—something she says she had wanted to
do to "that whole courtroom." Joel makes much of the fact that a
turning point in the trial occurred on "8/8/08," which he claims has
some biblical numerological significance. At a small group meeting (very small, about twelve people in a room with 108 seats) I
attended on Saturday evening, the speaker endorsed the Jewish
dietary laws, or at least the avoidance of pork and shellfish, although most Christians believe that these laws were lifted two
thousand years ago by Peter and Paul. But where is Christianity
in all this? Where is the demand for humility and sacrificial love
for others? Where in particular is the Jesus who said, "If a man
sue you at law and take your coat, let him have your cloak also"?

Even God plays only a supporting role, and by no means an indispensable one, in the Osteens' universe. Gone is the mystery and
awe; he has been reduced to a kind of majordomo or personal as-

sistant. He fixeth my speeding tickets, he secureth me a good table in the restaurant, he leadeth me to book contracts. Even in these minor tasks, the invocation of God seems more of courtesy than a necessity. Once you have accepted the law of attraction—that the mind acts as a magnet attracting whatever it visualizes—you have granted humans omnipotence.

All of these departures from the Christian tradition have already been noted with shocked disapproval—by Christians. My Baptist friends in Houston can only shake their heads in dismay at Osteen's self-serving theology. On scores of Christian Web sites, you can find Osteen and other positive pastors denounced as "heretics," "false Christians," even as associates of the devil, sometimes on highly technical grounds (Joyce Meyer has put forth the idiosyncratic view that Jesus served time in hell to spare us from that experience), but more often for the obvious reasons: they put Mammon over God; they ignore the reality of sin; they reduce God to a servant of man; they trivialize a spiritually demanding religious tradition. On a 2007 *60 Minutes* segment on Osteen, a theology professor, Reverend Michael Horton, dismissed Osteen's worldview as "a cotton candy gospel" that omits Christianity's ancient and powerful themes of sin, suffering, and redemption. As for the central notion of positive theology—that God stands ready to give you anything you want—Horton describes this as "heresy," explaining that "it makes religion about us instead of about God."

Secular Roots

Whatever decorative touches positive preaching retains from the Christian tradition, its genealogy can be traced more or less directly to nineteenth-century New Thought. New Thought has its own extant denominations, like Christian Science and the smaller Unity Church, which arose in 1891 and, like Christian Science, was based on Phineas Parkhurst Quimby's teachings. Kansas pastor Will Bowen, author of *A Complaint Free World* and inventor of the purple complaint-free wristband, is a Unity minister, as is Edwene Gaines, who illustrates in her book, *The Four Pillars of Prosperity*, a breathtakingly bossy attitude toward God. When the two hundred dollars she needed for a plane ticket failed to materialize, she writes, "I sat down and gave God a severe talking-to. I said, 'Now look here, God! . . . As far as I know, I've done every single thing that I know to do in order to manifest this trip to Mexico City. I've kept my part of the bargain. So now I'm going to go right down to that travel agent and when I get there, that money had better be there!'"[12]

Other streams feeding into modern positive theology can also be traced, ultimately, to the teachings of that nineteenth-century Maine clockmaker Phineas Quimby. Norman Vincent Peale, as we have seen, drew on New Thought sources, and his most prominent successor today is Robert Schuller, who in 1958 enlisted Peale himself to help build up the congregation of Schuller's Crystal Cathedral. Like Peale, Schuller teaches a form of mental reprogramming based on visualization, affirmation, and repetition, only he marks it as his own by calling it "possibility thinking" instead of "positive thinking." But by the 1960s and 1970s, a diverse group of pastors were finding their way to New Thought without any help from Peale. Kenneth Hagin, considered the father of the Word of Faith movement, sometimes called "Word Faith" or the "prosperity gospel," derived his ideas from the work of the late-nineteenth- and early-twentieth-century evangelist E. W. Kenyon, whose ideas in turn have been painstakingly traced back to secular New Thought by D. R. McConnell.[13] Among Hagin's acolytes were Joel Osteen's father, John Osteen, as well as the first African American televangelist, Fred Price. Introduced to Hagin's work by a friend, Price later wrote, "I went home that night and read every single book [by Hagin] and I was changed forever. It was like the scales came off my eyes."[14] The Word of Faith message resonated powerfully with African Americans, who were eager to see the gains of the civil rights movement transformed into upward mobility. Another prominent prosperity preacher was the Harlem-based Frederick Eikerenkoetter, or "Reverend Ike," who had been a traditional fundamentalist until the midsixties, when he discovered what he called "Mind Science," derived from his reading of New Thought literature.[15] Sporting an enormous pompadour, he taught that poverty resulted from a wrong attitude and proved the correctness of his own thinking by acquiring a fleet of Cadillacs appointed in mink.

Contemporary Word of Faith preachers encourage a sense of brash entitlement, as in this commercial for the Atlanta-based Creflo Dollar's videotape series *Laying Hold of Your Inheritance: Getting What's Rightfully Yours*, described by religious scholar Milmon Harrison:

> "Yo quiero lo mio!" a young Hispanic woman unflinchingly demands. She seems to be looking right at me across the distance between her as a televised image and me as a bleary-eyed, early-Sunday-morning-before-church channel surfer. "I want my stuff—*RIGHT NOW!*" a professionally dressed African American man demands, bouncing boxer-style on his toes for extra emphasis. An African American woman signs the phrase with an intensity that mirrors that of the spoken words. So forcefully do they convey a sense of authority and *urgency* as they lay their claim to their "stuff" that I find myself caught up in the collective effervescence of the moment. It is all I can do to keep myself from adding mine to their

chorus of voices. "YEAH, I WANT MY STUFF
RIGHT NOW, TOO!"[16]

Mary Baker Eddy would not have put it so baldly, but she had articulated this vision of an all-giving God, or universe, just waiting
for our orders, more than a century earlier.

With Christian Science and the Unity Church, positive thinking had carved out a home within American Protestantism more
than a hundred years ago. So why did it suddenly became such a
prominent force at the end of the twentieth century? One possible
explanation is simple contagion: churches are influenced by secular trends, and certainly by the 1990s there was no dodging the
positive thinking available in the business literature, the self-help
books, and even weight-loss plans. Joel Osteen, for example, might
have picked up the tenets of positive thinking from his father or in
conversations with Houston businessmen or from any number of
books available in the business sections of airport bookstores.
Most observers agree, though, that there has been a trend *within*
Protestantism that increasingly disposes it toward the old New
Thought, and that trend is the "church growth movement." Starting in the eighties and accelerating in the last two decades, churches
have increasingly sacrificed doctrinal tradition to embrace growth
for its own sake, and positive thinking turns out to be a crucial
catalyst for growth. Of the four largest megachurches in the United
States, three offer the "prosperity gospel."[17] The other, Rick Warren's Saddleback Church, although hostile to the crass prosperity
gospel, is definitely within the positive theology camp—long on
"purpose" and opportunity, short on sin and redemption.

Corporate Churches

Size has always been a criterion for the success of a faith, although not the only one. Especially in the mainstream denominations, ministers seemed content for years to preach the same gospel, in the same church building, accompanied by the same music, even if this meant an increasing concentration on burying a dying congregation. The decline of mainstream church membership in the latter part of the twentieth century prodded a new generation of self-styled "pastorpreneurs" to try a fresh approach based on "strategic thinking" and "the aggressive goals of business."[18] Looking out on the American suburbs, they felt like missionaries facing a heathen population. Here were millions of people who professed to be believers yet remained "unchurched." In the "church growth movement" that had begun to emerge in the midfifties, energetic pastors drew on the experience of real missionaries in places like India, asking themselves, in effect, "How can we make our religion more congenial to the natives?" or, in the American setting, "What does it take to fill our parking lots?" To critics of growth for its own sake, and there are many—see, for example, the series "Is Church Growth the Highway to Hell?" on the Web site Church Marketing Sucks—an Atlanta Baptist church responded in a pamphlet: "A church gets big because its spirit is big. . . . Nobody ever started a business without hoping that someday, if he or she worked hard enough, it would be a big success. That is the American dream, isn't it?"[19]

In the new business-oriented approach to Christianity, you didn't start by opening a church and hoping that people would be drawn in by newspaper announcements of the services. You started by finding out what people *wanted* from a church. Pastors Robert Schuller, Rick Warren, and Bill Hybels did the groundwork for their megachurches by conducting surveys of potential parishioners, and what they found was that people did not want "church," or at least anything like the church they had experienced in childhood. If this were corporate market research, the company might have thrown up its hands and decided to abandon the product line, but enterprising pastors concluded that they simply had to reconfigure the old product. Hard pews were replaced with comfortable theater seats, sermons were interspersed with music, organs were replaced with guitars. And in a remarkable concession to the tastes of the unchurched—or, as they are also called, "seekers"—the megachurches by and large scuttled all the icons and symbols of conventional churches—crosses, steeples, and images of Jesus. Crosses, in particular, according to religious historian Randall Balmer, might affect the unchurched as they do vampires: they could "intimidate or frighten visitors."[20]

To further assuage the theophobia of the public, megachurches are typically designed to fit seamlessly into the modernist corporate-style environment that they inhabit. Gothic cathedrals were designed to counter the mundane world with a vision of transcendence, and to engage the imagination with the rich details of their ornamentation. The Protestant Reformation threw out the gargoyles and images of tortured saints but retained, in church design, a clean-lined rebuke to the secular world. Not so the megachurches, which seem bent on camouflaging themselves as suburban banks or school buildings. Surveying megachurches in 2005, the architect and writer Wytold Rybczynski found them, like Lakewood, "resolutely secular" in design. He wrote of Willow Creek Community Church, outside Chicago, for example, that "it doesn't look like a place of worship, but what does it look like? A performing-arts center, a community college, a corporate headquarters? . . . Inspiring it's not. It's the architectural equivalent of the three-piece business suit that most nondenominational pastors favor."[21]

And that is apparently the desired result—to "lower the threshold between the church and the secular world," as journalist Frances Fitzgerald writes, and reassure the "seeker" that he or she has not stumbled into some spiritual dimension different from that occupied by the standard bank or office building. To the Christian artist Bruce Bezaire, that is precisely what's wrong with corporate-style churches: "While we might legitimately contemplate the degradation of a culture's sense of Beauty when it has turned away from God, I'm concerned about the church's understanding of God when it has turned away from Beauty. What does stepping into a gray drywall box contribute to our experience of reverence, joy, exaltation, worship?"[22] But for others, the corporate camouflage seems to work. A member of the Lakewood congregation, a semiretired schoolteacher, told me that because she had been forced to go to Catholic school as a child and "hated everything about it," she was completely comfortable in the visually desolate environment of Lakewood, adding, "Church is not a building, it's in your heart."

When pastors surveyed their catchment areas, they found that what people *did* want was entertainment—rock or rocklike music, for example—and they wanted an array of services like child care and support for people dealing with divorce, addiction, or difficult teenagers. Missionary churches in the Third World had long ago learned to attract people with bits of local music and culture, as well as with church-affiliated schools and health services. In line with consumer demand, today's megachurches are multiservice centers offering pre- and after-school programs, sports, teen activities, recovery programs, employment help, health fairs, support groups for battered women and people going through divorce, even aerobics classes and weight-lifting rooms. American churches—mega and not so mega—have filled in with the kinds of services that might, in more generous nations, be provided by the secular welfare state.

But megachurch pastors took a further step that no missionary would have contemplated. A missionary might have accommodated to the local population with stylistic changes and the addition of social services, but only as a means to preach the "word," the core beliefs of Christianity regarding sin and salvation. Even in the interest of attracting more parishioners, he would not have gone so far as to adopt reincarnation or the notion of plural deities. Not so the pastorpreneurs, who have been willing to abandon traditional Christian teachings insofar as they might be overly challenging or disturbing. One thing that church market research revealed was that people definitely did not want to be harangued about sin and made to feel in any way bad about themselves. If you have only one day a week not given over to work or errands and laundry, you probably do not want to spend even an hour of it being warned of imminent punishment in hell. Megachurches and those aspiring to that status needed a substitute for the more demanding core of Christian teachings, and that has been, for the most part, positive thinking—not because it is biblically "true" or supported by scripture but because it produces satisfied "customers"— as some megachurch pastors refer to them—like the megachurch member who told the *Christian Science Monitor*, "We love it. We don't miss a Sunday. The message is always very positive and the music is great."[23] Most positive preachers see no tension between their message and traditional Christian doctrine. God is good, so he wants the best for us, or, as Joyce Meyer puts it, "I believe God wants to give us nice things."[24]

A positive message not only sold better to the public than the "old-time religion" but also had a growing personal relevance to pastors, who increasingly came to see themselves not as critics of the secular, materialistic world but as players within it—businessmen or, more precisely, CEOs. This is not an idle conceit. While old-style churches—"minichurches," perhaps we should call them—

handled budgets in the low six-figure range, megachurches take in and spend millions of dollars a year and employ hundreds of people, making their pastors the equivalent of many CEOs in the sheer scale of the enterprises they head up. Size alone dictates a businesslike approach to church management, and most mega-church pastors took their organizational model directly from the corporate playbook. For example, the *Economist* reports that at Bill Hybels's Willow Creek Community Church:

> The corporate theme is not just a matter of appear-ances. Willow Creek has a mission statement ("to turn irreligious people into fully devoted followers of Jesus Christ") and a management team, a seven-step strategy and a set of ten core values. The church em-ploys two MBAs—one from Harvard and one from Stanford—and boasts a consulting arm. It has even been given the ultimate business accolade: it is the subject of a Harvard Business School case-study.[25]

Megachurch pastors may even consort with real CEOs and be flattered to think of themselves as companions to these hard-headed men of the world. Rick Warren of the Saddleback Church has been mingling with the "masters of the universe" at Davos for years, and in a *New Yorker* article Malcolm Gladwell quoted him as saying:

> "I had dinner with Jack Welch last Sunday night. . . . He came to church, and we had dinner. I've been kind of mentoring him on his spiritual journey. And he said to me, 'Rick, you are the biggest thinker I have ever met in my life. The only other person I know who thinks globally like you is Rupert Murdoch.' And

I said, 'That's interesting. I'm Rupert's pastor! Rupert
published my book!'" Then he tilted back his head
and gave one of those big Rick Warren laughs.[26]

The top pastors no doubt look to Jesus for guidance, at least
they freely invoke his name, but they also look to secular management consultants and gurus. In his book *PastorPreneur*, Reverend John Jackson cites the positive-thinking guru Stephen
Covey. Bill Hybels is an admirer of Peter Drucker and, at least as
of 1995, had a poster hanging just outside his office quoting the
questions that management expert urged businesspeople to ask
themselves: "What is our business? Who is our customer? What
does the customer consider value?" There are plenty of Christian-
oriented "church growth" consultancies for pastors to turn to
also; in fact, a small industry has arisen to advise aspiring pastors on everything from parking lots to events management, and
some of the more successful megachurches, like Saddleback and
Willow Creek, have spawned ancillary businesses as church growth
consultancies themselves, offering training seminars, Web sites,
and conferences for the pastors of lesser churches. But no one denies the role of secular inspiration in megachurches—if the distinction between sacred and secular even makes sense here. Robert
Schuller likes to include celebrity guests in his services, and they
have included well-known motivational speakers and the CEO
of Amway. As one ambitious pastor told the *New York Times*:
"Corporations are teaching us to look to the future and dream
dreams."[27]

The more pastors functioned as CEOs, socialized with CEOs,
and immersed themselves in the lore of corporate management,
the more they were likely to think of themselves as fellow CEOs.
Business leaders needed to think positively in order to sell their
products and increase their market share; so too did enterprising

pastors. A growing number of them are nondenominational, meaning they cannot turn to a centralized bureaucracy for financial or
any other kind of support. Facing uncharted territory and a skeptical population of the unchurched, they depend entirely on their
own charisma and salesmanship, which in turn often depends on
positive thinking. Osteen, for example, attributes his acquisition
of the Compaq Center not only to God but also to his ability to
visualize this bold move: "I began to 'see' our congregation wor-
shiping God in the Compaq Center in the heart of Houston." He
advises anyone interested in prosperity to do the same: "Get rid of
those old wineskins. Get rid of that small-minded thinking and
start thinking as God thinks. Think big. Think increase. Think
abundance. Think more than enough."[28]

Churches are not the only institutions to have become more
"corporate" in recent decades, in their appearance, management,
and techniques for growth. Universities have been corporatized,
hiring MBAs as administrators, evolving from Gothic to blank
modernist design, adopting aggressive marketing techniques, and,
as noted earlier, occasionally bringing in motivational speakers. At
a meeting of another kind of nonprofit a few years ago—one devoted to expanding women's economic opportunities—I was sur-
prised to find it "facilitated" by a hired team-building coach who
had us start by breaking into small groups to "bond" over our
dreams and "most embarrassing experiences." Even labor unions,
the historic antagonists of corporations, are likely today to employ
corporate styles of management and—what would have been un-
thinkable to the kind of old-fashioned organizer who struck up
conversations with workers in bars or at factory gates—to use surveys and focus groups to shape their appeals to potential recruits.
Everywhere you go, you are likely to encounter the same corporate
jargon of "incentivizing," "value added," and "going forward"; the
same chains of command; the same arrays of desks and cubicles;

the same neutral, functionalist disregard for aesthetics; the same reliance on motivation and manufactured team spirit.

But it could be argued that a special affinity has grown up between corporations and the churches, especially megachurches, that goes beyond superficial similarities. In the last couple of decades, while churches were becoming more like corporations, corporations were becoming more like churches—headed up by charismatic figures claiming, or aspiring to, almost mystical powers of leadership. Commenting on the trend toward charismatic, or, as they call it, "transformational" leadership, two management professors have written that "much management practice is indeed moving beyond a purely metaphorical similarity to the rituals and mindsets of religious devotion." They argue that corporations increasingly resemble what are commonly known as cults—organizations that demand total acquiescence to a seemingly divinely inspired leader.[29] Not only have megachurch pastors taken corporate CEOs as role models, but CEOs have sometimes returned the favor, as in the mutual admiration between Rick Warren and his CEO friends. In an article on the megachurch phenomenon, the *Economist* noted:

> Indeed, in a nice reversal businesses have also started to learn from the churches. The late Peter Drucker pointed out that these churches have several lessons to teach mainline businesses. They are excellent at motivating their employees and volunteers, and at transforming volunteers from well-meaning amateurs into disciplined professionals. The best churches (like some of the most notorious cults) have discovered the secret of low-cost and self-sustaining growth: transforming seekers into evangelicals who will then go out and recruit more seekers.[30]

So, from a seeker's point of view, what *is* the difference between a megachurch and the corporation at which he or she works? Visually, not much: the megachurch looks like a corporate office building or headquarters; its pastor is more likely to wear a business suit than clerical robes; religious symbols and icons have been stripped away. In addition, both institutions offer, as their core philosophy, a motivational message about getting ahead, overcoming obstacles, and achieving great things through positive thinking. To further enhance the connection between church and workplace, some leading pastors make a point of endorsing "free enterprise" and its demands on the average worker. Schuller warns against using the fact of being "disadvantaged" or subjected to racial prejudice as "an excuse to keep from trying."[31] Osteen writes that "employers prefer employees who are excited about working at their companies," and to those who feel they're not paid enough to feel "excited," he counsels: "You won't be blessed, with that kind of attitude. God wants you to give it everything you've got. Be enthusiastic. Set an example."[32]

But there's one immediately obvious difference between the megachurch and the corporate workplace: church is *nice*. No one will yell at you, impose impossible deadlines, or make you feel inadequate. Smiling volunteers greet you as you enter on Sunday morning, and after the service you may get to shake the CEO's— that is, the pastor's—hand. There is child care, as well as all the support groups and services. Best of all, even if you fail to tithe at the generally recommended 10 percent, even if you are guilty of frequent absenteeism or lack the time to volunteer, even if you lapse back into what was once known as sin and now understood as "negativity," you will not be asked to leave. And this may be an important part of the megachurches' appeal: they are simulacra of the corporate workplace, offering all the visual signs of corporate power and efficiency, only without the cruelty and fear. You cannot be downsized from church.

So the seeker who embraces positive theology finds him- or herself in a seamless, self-enclosed world, stretching from workplace to mall to corporate-style church. Everywhere, he or she hears the same message—that you *can* have all that stuff in the mall, as well as the beautiful house and car, if only you believe that you can. But always, in a hissed undertone, there is the darker message that if you don't have all that you want, if you feel sick, discouraged, or defeated, you have only yourself to blame. Positive theology ratifies and completes a world without beauty, transcendence, or mercy.

SIX

Positive Psychology:
The Science of Happiness

It was 1997, and Martin Seligman anxiously awaited the results of an electoral drama little noted by the rest of the nation—the choice of a new president for the American Psychological Association. A distinguished researcher and skilled organizational player within the APA, Seligman was nevertheless convinced that he would lose. By his own admission, he is a "dyed-in-the-wool pessimist," a "grouch," even a "walking nimbus cloud."[1] But apparently unharmed by his negativity, he won and within a few months proposed that the theme of his presidency would be "positive psychology"—the study of "positive" emotions and mind-sets like optimism, happiness, fulfillment, and "flow."

Until Seligman's ascendency within the psychology profession, positive thinking had gained no purchase in the academy. In the fifties, intellectuals mocked Norman Vincent Peale, and four decades later academics tended to dismiss the ideas of his successors as pop cultural ephemera and the stuff of cheap hucksterism.

But when Seligman secured a bully pulpit—and set about attracting a rich, nurturing stream of foundation money—respectable
Ph.D.-level psychologists began to generate a huge volume of academic papers, some of them published in the new *Journal of Happiness Studies*, linking optimism and happiness to every possible
desirable outcome, including health and career success. The new
positive psychology, or "science of happiness," was an instant hit
with the media, winning cover stories in news magazines and a
steady drumbeat of good news (for optimists, anyway) in the newspapers. For any nonacademic motivational speaker, coach, or self-
help entrepreneur who happened to be paying attention, it was a
godsend. No longer did they need to invoke the deity or occult notions like the law of attraction to explain the connection between
positive thoughts and positive outcomes; they could fall back on
that touchstone phrase of rational, secular discourse—"studies
show . . ."

Positive psychologists are usually careful to distance themselves from the pop versions of positive thinking. "We see it as so
different from what we do," one academic happiness researcher—
Stanford's Sonja Lyubomirsky—told *Elle* magazine, "like, 'Well,
we do science, and those people are just spouting off their ideas.'"
In the same article, Seligman dismissed pop positive thinking as
"fraudulent" and promised that, within a decade, "we'll have self-
help books that actually work."[2] Positive psychologists do not
subscribe to the law of attraction or promise to make their readers
rich. In fact, they have a certain contempt for wealth—not un-
common among academics—and focus instead on the loftier goal
of *happiness* and all the benefits, such as health, that it supposedly
confers.

But the positive psychologists have been quick to borrow from
the playbook of their cousins in the coaching and motivation

businesses. They publish mass-market books with "you" or "your" in the title—a tell-tale sign of the self-help genre—like Seligman's *What You Can Change . . . and What You Can't* and *Authentic Happiness: Using the New Positive Psychology to Realize Your Potential for Lasting Fulfillment*. They go into the life-coaching business— as Seligman did, for example, until 2005, providing coaching by conference call to hundreds of people at a time for $2,000 each. He also developed a cash-generating Web site, reflectivehappiness .com, promoting "monthly exercises intended to increase happiness," which came with the hucksterish assurance that "we are so confident that this program will help you, we've developed a no-obligation, limited-time offer to try Dr. Seligman's powerful program for one month free."[3]

And, following the motivation industry, positive psychologists have reached out to claim a market in the corporate world. The 2007 book *Positive Psychology Coaching: Putting the Science of Happiness to Work for Your Clients* admits that "the idea of selling happiness to large companies might seem preposterous" but quickly goes on to list the bottom-line benefits of happiness in the form of more eager and productive workers, eventually concluding that "happiness doesn't need to be sold. . . . It sells itself."[4] Seligman himself consulted to the management of David's, a chain of bridal shops, reportedly generating increased sales, as well as to unnamed Fortune 500 companies, offering "exercises" to increase employees' optimism and hence, supposedly, their health.[5]

Whatever it was—scientific breakthrough or flamboyant bid for funding and attention—positive psychology provided a solution to the mundane problems of the psychology profession. Effective antidepressants had become available at the end of the 1980s, and these could be prescribed by a primary care physician after a ten-minute diagnostic interview, so what was left for a psychologist to do? In the 1990s, managed care providers and insurance companies turned against traditional psychotherapy, effectively defunding those practitioners who offered lengthy courses of talk therapy. The Michigan Psychological Association declared psychology "a profession at risk" and a California psychologist told the *San Francisco Chronicle* that "because of managed care, many clinical psychologists aren't being allowed to treat clients as they believe they should. They still want to work in the field of helping people, so they're moving out of therapy into coaching."[6] If there was no support for treating the sick, there were endless possibilities in coaching ordinary well people in the direction of greater happiness, optimism, and personal success. "Lying awake at night," Seligman wrote in his introduction to his book *Authentic Happiness*, "you probably ponder, as I have, how to go from plus two to plus seven in your life, not just how to go from minus five to minus three."[7]

Seligman did not, of course, present the shift away from a "negative," pathology-oriented psychology as a new career strategy for psychologists. He spoke of it as a response to historical circumstances, telling an interviewer in 2000—perhaps forgivably, since this was before the bursting of the dot-com bubble, 9/11, and war with Iraq—that:

> It is surprising that we have very high levels of depression and pessimism in a world in which the hands on the nuclear clock are farther away from midnight than they have ever been, in a nation in which every economic indicator, every objective indicator of well-being, is going north, in a world in which there are fewer soldiers dying on the battlefield than any time since WWII, and in which there is a lower percentage

of children dying of starvation than at any time in
human history.[8]

Why so much negativity in such a comfortable age? Seligman
blames our perilous evolution: "Because our brain evolved during
a time of ice, flood and famine, we have a catastrophic brain. The
way the brain works is looking for what's wrong. The problem is,
that worked in the Pleistocene era. It favored you, but it doesn't
work in the modern world."[9] As he wrote in 2004 with his frequent collaborator Ed Diener, "Because goods and services are
plentiful and because simple needs are largely satisfied in modern
societies, people today have the luxury of refocusing their attention on the 'good life.'"[10] In this view, which was restated uncriti-
cally by a reviewer of two books on happiness in a February 2006
issue of the New Yorker, our Paleolithic ancestors may have been
well served by the suspicion that a saber-toothed cat crouched
behind every bush, but today we would do better to visualize pots
of gold.[11]

Going to the Source

I approached my chance to interview Martin Seligman in May
2007 with some trepidation. Only three months earlier I had published an essay in Harper's critical of both positive psychology
and pop positive thinking. Sure enough, when I first encountered
Seligman he was practically scowling. "There he is!" the security
guard at the reception desk in a boxlike building at the University
of Pennsylvania said, pointing upward to a short, solid, bullet-
headed man looking down from the second-floor balcony. I smiled
and waved, to which Seligman responded only, "You'll have to
take the elevator."

He was not, however, waiting for me on the second floor and had disappeared into his office. His secretary informed me that he would be busy for a minute and that he wanted me to meet these two ladies from the Australian military while I waited. After shaking their hands and learning that they had come for help in "preventing problems before they get to the complaint stage," I was ushered into his office, only to face another delay—a phone call from the BBC, he told me, which I was welcome to sit through, although no chair was offered.

The phone call—to schedule an interview about a plan to offer "optimism training" in the British public schools—seemed to lift his spirits, and after a few minutes of innocuous conversation, he announced that it was such a beautiful day that it would be a shame to spend it indoors. "I have a plan," he said. "We're going to go the art museum. Flowers will be blooming outdoors and we can see the Monets." I protested weakly that this excursion might interfere with note taking, not bothering to point out the contradiction between being in a museum and being outdoors. But apparently he was following his own instruction from *Authentic Happiness*: "Choose your venue and design your mood to fit the task at hand."[12] As soon as we were in a taxi heading to the museum, he revealed that the Monets were his wife's idea. "That'll put her in a good mood," she had suggested. I began to wonder whether the Australian visitors and the BBC call had been timed, in part, for my benefit.

Once we were at the museum—the one made famous by Rocky Balboa—the barriers to a normal interview seemed only to multiply. First he insisted on a quick tramp around the outside of the building; then, inside at the reception desk, he made my heart sink by inquiring about a lecture that seemed to be going on. When that turned out to be unavailable, he started asking about an exhibition of photographs of early Santa Monica, and I pic-

tured an afternoon spent trailing him throughout the more ob-
scure sections of the museum. It was impossible not to dwell on
the fact that Seligman's early work, before he announced the
launching of positive psychology, had been about "learned helplessness," showing that when dogs are tormented in random ways
they become passive, depressed, and unable to defend themselves.

Although note taking was almost impossible, I attempted to
carry on a conversation about *Authentic Happiness*, which I had
found just as elusive as he was turning out to be. Like most lay
books on positive thinking, it's a jumble of anecdotes (primarily
autobiographical in Seligman's case), references to philosophers
and religious texts, and tests you can take to assess your progress
toward a happier and healthier mind-set. Only on a second reading did I begin to discern a progression of thoughts—not a logical
progression but at least a kind of arc. He begins with what positive
psychologists call their field's "origin story," about how he was
weeding his garden one day when his five-year-old daughter challenged him to stop being such a "grouch." Grouchiness, he realizes,
is endemic to the academic world: "I have noticed over thirty years
of psychology department faculty meetings—conducted in a cheer-
less, gray, and windowless room full of unrepentant grouches—
that the ambient mood is on the chilly side of zero." Prodded
by his daughter, he decides that "it was worth trying hard to put
more positive emotion into my life," and a veritable candy land of
pleasures begins to open up, epitomized by "a cloudless spring day,
the ending of the Beatles' 'Hey Jude,' pictures of babies and young
lambs, and sitting down in front of a blazing fire on a snowy
evening."[13]

But just as he seems to be on the verge of embracing hedonism,
or at least a kitschy version thereof, he pulls back sharply in a
burst of Calvinist disgust, enjoining the reader to "strive for

more gratifications, while toning down the pursuit of pleasure."
"Gratifications," it turns out, are "higher" forms of pleasure because they take some effort, and they include "playing three sets
of tennis, or participating in a clever conversation, or reading
Richard Russo." In contrast, things like "watching a sitcom, mas-
turbating, and inhaling perfume" involve no challenge and hence
are only "pleasures." This seems unnecessarily judgmental, and
not only because Richard Russo is not exactly Marcel Proust, but
the reader soon finds, to her complete confusion, that the whole
category of "positive emotions," including both gratification and
pleasure, is suspect: "When an entire lifetime is taken up in the
pursuit of positive emotions, however, authenticity and meaning
are nowhere to be found," and without them, evidently, there can
be no "authentic happiness."[14]

Abandoning the positive emotions, Seligman's book goes off
in search of "character," which he admits is a Calvinist-sounding
concept—"nineteenth-century Protestant, constipated, and Vic-
torian." To get to the roots of character, he and his colleagues sift
through two hundred "virtue catalogs"—including Aristotle and
Plato, Augustine and Aquinas, the Old Testament, Confucius,
Buddha, and Benjamin Franklin—out of which they distill "six
virtues": wisdom and knowledge, courage, love and humanity,
justice, temperance, spirituality and transcendence.[15] Now, as we
walked up the museum stairs to the Monet exhibition, I told him
that he had lost me at this point in his book. Courage, for example, could take one very far from the "positive emotions," with
their predicted positive effects on health and success, and into
dangerous and painful situations, just as spirituality could lead to
social withdrawal, fasting, and self-mortification. In fact, I blath-
ered on, the conventional notion of "character" seems to include
the capacity for self-denial, even suffering, in pursuit of a higher
goal. To my surprise, he deflected the implicit criticism onto his

erstwhile collaborator, Ed Diener, saying that Diener is "all about the smiley face" and just "trying to make people feel better," whereas he, Seligman, is concerned with "meaning and purpose." Loyalty, I recall, did not make it onto the list of virtues.

Finally we arrived at the Monets, where after some preliminary gushing on his part we sat down on a bench and I settled my stenographer's pad on my knee for some serious interviewing. But just then a security guard bore down on us and announced that I could not use a pen in the presence of the Monets. It is true, I don't like the Monets, if only because they have been so thoroughly absorbed—along with lavender, scones, and "pictures of babies and young lambs"—into middle-class notions of coziness. I wanted to protest that I don't hate them enough to stab them with my felt-tip pen, but I obediently traded it in for one of the stubby No. 2 pencils available at a nearby desk. At this point, the interview seemed to have gotten completely out of control: Seligman was the psychologist; I was the mental patient, deprived of sharp objects.

I plowed ahead, focusing now on the "Authentic Happiness Inventory," a test available on one of his Web sites (http://www .authentichappiness.sas.upenn.edu). I had scored a less-than-jubilant 3.67 out of 5, and one of the questions that had pulled down my score asked the test taker to choose between "A. I am ashamed of myself" and "E. I am extraordinarily proud of myself." I am neither of these, and since we'd been talking about virtues, it seemed fair to ask: "Isn't pride a sin?" He answered that "it may be bad, but it has a high predictive value." Predictive of what—health? "The research is not fine-grained enough to say that pride predicts health." Frustrated and by now utterly baffled, I moved on to another question that had hurt my score, where I had confessed to being "pessimistic about the future," assuming that it was the future of our species at issue, not just my own. Now, in the museum,

I mentioned the possibilities of specieswide disasters like extinction or barbarism, but he just looked at me intently and said that, if I could "learn" optimism, as in his earlier book *Learned Optimism: How to Change Your Mind and Your Life,* which shows the reader how to reprogram his or her thoughts in a more optimistic direction, my productivity as a writer would soar.

Only when we returned to his office, away from the mood-elevating Monets, did things take a nasty turn. Going back to his Authentic Happiness Inventory, I remarked that many of the questions seemed a bit arbitrary, leading him to snap, "That's a cheap shot and shows your failure to understand test development. It doesn't matter what the questions are so long as they have predictive value. It could be a question about butterscotch ice cream and whether you like it. The issue is how well it predicts." Well, no. First you come up with a test that seems to measure happiness as generally defined, and then you can look for things that happiness seems to correlate with, such as liking butterscotch ice cream. But you cannot fold the ice cream into the definition of happiness itself.

Instead of saying this, I moved on to one of the most irritatingly pseudoscientific assertions in his book, the "happiness equation," which he introduces with the coy promise that it "is the only equation I ask you to consider," as if positive psychology rests on whole thickets of equations from which the reader will mercifully be spared.[16] The equation is:

$$H=S+C+V$$

H is "your enduring level of happiness, S is your set range, C is the circumstances of your life, and V represents factors under your voluntary control," such as, for example, whether you engage in "optimism training" to suppress negative or pessimistic thoughts. I understand what he is trying to say: that a person's

happiness is determined in some way by his or her innate dispo-
sition (S), immediate circumstances (C), like a recent job loss or
bereavement, and by the efforts (V) that the person makes to
improve his or her outlook. This could be stated unobjection-
ably as:

$$H = f(S, C, V)$$

Or, in words: H is a function of S, C, V, where the exact nature
of that function is yet to be determined. But to express it as an
equation is to invite ridicule. I asked the question that would oc-
cur to any first-year physics student: "What are the units of measurement?" Because if you're going to add these things up you will
have to have the same units for H (happy thoughts per day?) as for
V, S, and C. "Well, you'd need some constant in front of each," he
said, and when I pressed on, he responded that "C is going to de-
compose into twenty different things, like religion and marriage,"
referring to the fact that positive psychologists have found that
married and religious people are likely to be happier than single
and skeptical people. So how, I ask, do you boil C into a single
number? Again, his face twisted into a scowl, and he told me that
I didn't understand "beta weighting" and should go home and
Google it.

So, just to be sure, I did, finding that "beta weights" are the co-
efficients of the "predictors" in a regression equation used to find
statistical correlations between variables. But Seligman had presented his formula as an ordinary equation, like $E = mc^2$, not as an
oversimplified regression analysis, leaving himself open to literal-
minded questions like: How do we know H is a simple sum of the
variables, rather than some more complicated relationship, possibly involving "second order" effects such as CV, or C times V?
But clearly Seligman wanted an equation, because equations add

a veneer of science, and he wanted it quickly, so he fell back on simple addition. No doubt equations make a book look weightier and full of mathematical rigor, but this one also makes Seligman look like the Wizard of Oz.

The field of psychology has produced its own critics of positive psychology, none more outspoken than Barbara Held, a professor at Bowdoin College. A striking woman with long black hair and a quick sense of humor, Held wrote her own self-help book, defiantly titled *Stop Smiling, Start Kvetching*. When she was invited to speak on a panel at the International Positive Psychology Summit in 2003, she arrived with T-shirts picturing a smiley face with a cancel sign through it and offered them to both Seligman and Diener. One of her major complaints centers on positive psychology's approval of "positive illusions" as a means to happiness and well-being. She quotes Seligman: "It is not the job of Positive Psychology to tell you that you should be optimistic, or spiritual, or kind or good-humored; it is rather to describe the consequences of these traits (for physical health, and higher achievement, *at a cost perhaps of less realism*)" (italics added).[17] If, as she writes, "positive psychologists of all stripes tout their dedication to rigorous science," how can they be prepared to toss out "realism and objectivity?" She argues that some positive psychologists are employing a "double epistemic standard," upholding objective and unbiased science while endorsing an "optimistic bias" in everyday life.[18]

Happiness and Health

The central claim of positive psychology, as of positive thinking generally, is that happiness—or optimism, positive emotions, positive affect, or positive *something*—is not only desirable in and of itself but actually useful, leading to better health and greater success. One book on positive psychology states that "happiness . . . is more than pleasant, it is beneficial," and Seligman begins *Authentic Happiness* by summarizing a few studies showing that happy (or positive) people live longer than unhappy ones.[19] In other words, you should make an effort to be happy, if only because the consequences of unhappiness may include poor health and lower achievement. Would happiness stop being an appealing goal if it turned out to be associated with illness and failure? Isn't it possible to imagine being gloriously contented with a life spent indulging unhealthy habits, like the proverbially happy "pigs in shit"? Nothing underscores the lingering Calvinism of positive psychology more than this need to put happiness to work—as a means to health and achievement, or what the positive thinkers call "success."

Happy, or positive, people—however that is measured—do seem to be more successful at work. They are more likely to get a second interview while job hunting, get positive evaluations from superiors, resist burnout, and advance up the career ladder. But this probably reflects little more than the corporate bias in favor of a positive attitude and against "negative" people. A widely cited review article entitled "The Benefits of Frequent Positive Affect: Does Happiness Lead to Success?," coauthored by Ed Diener, makes no mention of this bias and hence appears to do little more than to confirm it.[20]

When it comes to the proposed health benefits of a positive outlook, the positive psychologists would seem to be on firmer ground. As we have seen, a positive outlook cannot cure cancer, but in the case of more common complaints, we tend to suspect that people who are melancholy, who complain a lot, or who ruminate obsessively about every fleeting symptom may in fact be making themselves sick. Recall the miraculous cures worked on chronic invalids by Phineas Quimby and others in the nineteenth century, simply by encouraging them to get up out of bed and start thinking of themselves as healthy people. We don't have "neurasthenics" today, but there are plenty of ills with a psychosomatic component, some of which may indeed yield to a "mind over matter" approach. When John E. Sarno, a professor of rehabilitation medicine, published a book proposing that lower back pain was caused by repressed anger rather than a physical abnormality and that it was curable by mental exercises, thousands testified that they were helped, including the well-known health guru Andrew Weil.[21]

In contrast to the flimsy research linking attitude to cancer survival, there are scores of studies showing that happy or optimistic people are likely to be healthier than those who are sour-tempered and pessimistic. Most of these studies, however, only establish correlations and tell us nothing about causality: Are people healthy because they're happy or happy because they're healthy? To sort out which comes first, you need longitudinal studies carried out over time. Three such studies are cited frequently by positive psychologists, and none is exactly airtight.

One, the 2001 "nun study," which Seligman calls "the most remarkable study of happiness and longevity ever done," purports to show that happier nuns live longer than less happy ones—into their nineties as opposed to their seventies or eighties.[22] The questionable thing here is the measure of happiness. In the early 1930s, when the nuns were about twenty-two years old, they had written brief sketches of their lives and commitment to the religious life. Some of these sketches contained a high "positive emotional content," as judged by the researchers, with statements such as "I look forward with eager joy to receiving the Holy Habit of Our Lady and to a life of union with Love Divine." As it turned out, the nuns who registered high in positive emotional content outlived the ones who had written such matter-of-fact statements as "with God's grace, I intend to do my best for our Order, for the spread of religion and for my personal sanctification." But since not everyone is capable of expressing their emotions vividly in writing, there's a leap between "positive emotional content" and subjective happiness. One might just as well conclude that the key to longevity lies in good writing, and an earlier study by one of the authors seemed to suggest just that: nuns who, in their youth, wrote complex sentences with high "idea density" turned out to be less likely to succumb to Alzheimer's disease in old age.[23]

A second longitudinal study, also cited by Seligman at the beginning of *Authentic Happiness*, does not even bear directly on the proposition that happiness leads to better health. In this case, happiness was measured by the apparent authenticity of smiles. Poring over the class photos in two mid-twentieth-century yearbooks for Mills College, a private liberal arts school for women, the researchers found that about half the young women smiled "authentically," with eyes crinkled and the corners of their mouths turned up, and that decades later these happy smilers reported being more happily married and generally satisfied with their lives. Whatever the relevance of this finding, it could not be replicated in a similar study of high school yearbook pictures from Wisconsin.[24] For the less elite population in the high school photos, happy smiles did not predict happy lives.

Finally, the positive psychologists like to cite a study of older Mexican Americans—sixty-five and up—that found that people who reported being happy were likely to live longer and experience less frailty than those who did not.[25] In *Authentic Happiness*, Seligman writes that this study, combined with the nun and Mills College studies, creates "an unambiguous picture of happiness as a prolonger of life and improver of health."[26] But even here, a question can be raised. The study controlled for income, education, weight, smoking, and drinking but not for physical activity, which is a known predictor of health and strength in old age. It could be that the happier Mexican Americans were healthier simply because they were more likely to walk, dance, exercise, or engage in physical labor—a possibility that one of the authors of the study tells me they are now looking into.

Adding further ambiguity to the "picture of happiness as a prolonger of life and improver of health" are a number of studies showing that happiness or other positive emotional states may have no effect on one's health. As we saw in chapter 1, an improved mental outlook—generated in support groups or through psychotherapy—does not extend the lives of breast cancer patients, and the same has been found for those suffering from throat and neck cancer. Nor, it turns out, does optimism add to the longevity of lung cancer patients.[27] The evidence that positive emotions can protect against coronary heart disease seems sturdier, although I am not in a position to evaluate it. At least a list of articles on heart disease and emotional states compiled for me by Seligman included a number of studies finding that optimism and other positive states can both protect against heart disease and hasten recovery from it.[28] But others on Seligman's list were more equivocal, and one study cited by Barbara Held found that people high in "trait negative affect" do more complaining about angina but are at no greater risk of pathology than cheerful people.[29]

Some of the studies Held has reviewed even conclude that negative traits like pessimism can be healthier in the long run than optimism and happiness.[30] For example, a 2002 study found that women who are mildly depressed are more likely to live longer than nondepressed or very depressed women. Somewhat alarmingly, a longitudinal study of more than a thousand California schoolchildren concluded that optimism was likely to lead to an earlier death in middle or old age, possibly because the optimistic people took more risks. Another, more recent, study found that preteenagers who were realistic about their standing among their peers were less likely to become depressed than those who held positive illusions about their popularity.[31] But the most surprising case for pessimism comes from a 2001 study coauthored by Seligman himself, finding that, among older people, pessimists were less likely to fall into depression following a negative life event such as the death of a family member.[32] This study goes unmentioned in *Authentic Happiness*, but at the time it led Seligman to comment to the *New York Times* that "it's important that optimism not be footless [probably meaning "footloose"] and unwarranted."[33] So realism has its uses after all.

But the results that go out to the public through the media tend to be spun toward the positive effects of positive emotions on health. Partly, this represents a long-standing media bias away from "null results": a study finding, for example, that there is no sex difference in the ability to sprint or solve quadratic equations is likely to be judged less newsworthy than a study reporting that one sex left the other in the dust. In the case of positive psychology, a 2002 *New York Times* article cited two studies linking optimism to longevity—and four studies tracing longevity to such other traits as "conscientiousness," calmness, pessimism, and even cantankerousness. Yet the article was headlined "Power of Positive Thinking Extends, It Seems, to Aging."[34] Some positive psychologists acknowledge the pressure to feed the media positive-sounding results, with the editors of the *Handbook of Positive Psychology* warning that:

> In the excitement that may be associated with this
> new and invigorating approach [positive psychology],
> it may be tempting to overextrapolate so as to convey
> a sense of the progress that is being made. This can be

even more possible when a person from the news media is almost putting words in our mouths about the
supposed discoveries and advances that already have
occurred.[35]

The positive spin on positive psychology cannot be blamed
entirely on overeager reporters. Consider a 2005 review article
entitled "Does Positive Affect Influence Health?," the summary of
which says in its entirety:

> This review highlights consistent patterns in the lit-
> erature associating positive affect (PA) and physical
> health. However, it also raises serious conceptual and
> methodological reservations. Evidence suggests an
> association of trait PA and lower morbidity and of
> state and trait PA and decreased symptoms and pain.
> Trait PA is also associated with increased longevity
> among older community-dwelling individuals. The
> literature on PA and surviving serious illness is in-
> consistent. Experimentally inducing intense bouts of
> activated state PA triggers short-term rises in physi-
> ological arousal and associated (potentially harmful)
> effects on immune, cardiovascular, and pulmonary
> function. However, arousing effects of state PA are
> not generally found in naturalistic ambulatory stud-
> ies in which bouts of PA are typically less intense and
> often associated with health protective responses. A
> theoretical framework to guide further study is pro-
> posed.[36]

Yet when asked in an interview to "summarize the significance of
your paper in layman's terms," the authors set aside all their "res-

ervations" and concerns about "inconsistent" literature and "potentially harmful" effects to respond cheerily that "the paper provides preliminary evidence that persons who more often experience positive emotions such as happiness, enthusiasm, and calmness, are less likely to develop a range of diseases, live longer, and experience fewer symptoms and less pain."[37]

Another case of positive self-spinning is provided by Suzanne Segerstrom, a researcher at the University of Kentucky, who won the 2002 Templeton Foundation Award for Positive Psychology for her work on what may be the holy grail of positive psychology—the possible link between positive emotions and the immune system. Although the immune system plays no clear role in cancer, it is definitely important in fighting off colds and other infectious illnesses. Whether there is a link between positive emotions and the immune system is another matter. Martin Seligman asserts such a link, writing that "happy people" have "feistier immune systems than less happy people." In a 1998 paper, Segerstrom reported that optimism was correlated with greater immune competence, as measured by levels of key immune cell types. But in a second study, published three years later, she found that "some contradictory findings have emerged" and that, in some circumstances, more optimistic people "fare worse immunologically" than pessimists.[38]

You would not know, however, that her results were negative or at best "mixed" from reading her newspaper accounts of her work. In a 2002 interview with the *New York Daily News*, she stated that the health benefits of optimism are "significant" and that not only do "optimists almost always have better emotional adjustments," but "most optimists show higher immune responses to illness."[39] When I interviewed Segerstrom by phone in 2007, she insisted that she had been under no pressure from the media, or anyone else, to downplay her negative results. But when I brought up her award a little later on in our talk, she told me, "To get the Templeton award . . . You don't get anything for a null result."

The Templeton Connection

The Templeton Foundation, which contributed $2.2 million to Seligman's Positive Psychology Center in the first decade of the twenty-first century, as well as about $1.3 million to miscellaneous positive-psychology research projects on such matters as gratitude, humility, and connectedness, is probably best known for its efforts to put religion on an equal intellectual footing with science. Founded by billionaire investor Sir John Templeton in 1972, the foundation gives out an annual Templeton Prize for Progress in Religion, which was designed to fill a gap left by the Nobel prizes and pointedly pays more than they do. (In 2002, perhaps reflecting a certain lack of progress in religion, it was renamed the Templeton Prize for Progress toward Research or Discoveries about Spiritual Realities.) The foundation's campaign to bring scientific legitimacy to religion has led to some dubious ventures, including funding in 1999 for a conference on intelligent design as an alternative to evolution. More cautiously, in recent years, the foundation has backed away from intelligent design and expressed its "spiritual" orientation through funding for research into the efficacy of prayer—another null result—as well as various abstract qualities like "character" and "humility." Until his death in 2008, Sir John Templeton was fond of bringing scientists and theologians together with the aim of finding common ground in luxurious tropical resorts.

Templeton might have been attracted to positive psychology's claim that positive emotions can influence physical health—a "mind over matter" proposition that can be found in just about any form of American spiritualism since the nineteenth century. But there is another, more intriguing connection. Templeton was an acolyte of Norman Vincent Peale and a minor positive-thinking guru himself. According to the Templeton Foundation's 2004 "Capabilities Report," he "credits Norman Vincent Peale's book, *The Power of Positive Thinking*, read 70 years ago, with making him realize that 'what I had become in my short lifetime was mainly dependent on my mental attitudes—a mental attitude of looking for the good will bring good to you; a mental attitude of giving love will bring love to you.' "[40] Templeton wrote a number of books in the self-help genre, some of them conveniently published by his foundation, including *The Templeton Plan: 21 Steps to Personal Success and Real Happiness, Worldwide Laws of Life: 200 Eternal Spiritual Principles*, and *Discovering the Laws of Life*. The last one came with an endorsement from Robert Schuller and an introduction by Norman Vincent Peale himself, who described Templeton as "the greatest layman of the Christian church in our time." Surely, the possibility that positive psychology might eventually provide scientific undergirding for positive thinking was not lost on Templeton.

But Templeton was not just another positive-thinking businessman. He was something of a political ideologue, as is, to an even greater degree, his son and, since 1995, successor at the foundation. John Templeton Jr. is a major Republican donor and activist, having helped fund a group called Let Freedom Ring, which worked to get out the evangelical vote for George Bush in 2004. In 2007, he contributed to Freedom's Watch, which paid for television commercials supporting the war in Iraq, often by conflating Iraq with al Qaeda. More recently, he supported the Romney and then the McCain campaigns for the presidency and was the second-largest individual donor to the campaign for California's Proposition 8, banning same-sex marriage.[41]

The foundation itself is, of course, nonpartisan but is strongly biased in favor of "free enterprise." Over the years, it has given cash awards to a number of conservative scholars, including Milton Friedman and Gertrude Himmelfarb, and grants to a long list of conservative organizations, including the Heritage Foundation, the Manhattan Institute, the Jesse Helms Center Foundation, the Federalist Society, and the National Association of Scholars, which is best known for its battle against "political correctness" and academic liberalism.[42] Another recipient, the Association of Private Enterprise Education, states on its Web site that "the danger is very real that demagogues, while reviling 'the rich,' will loot the private wealth that is society's seed corn. The defense against demagogues is understanding and commitment to the principles of private enterprise. These are abstract principles and are not readily obvious." In its 2006 report, we learn that the Templeton Foundation "supports a wide range of programs and research initiatives to study the benefits of competition, specifically how free enterprise and other principles of capitalism can, and do, benefit the poor."[43] The words "and do" suggest a foregone conclusion, although the report goes on to raise the plaintive question "*Why should half the world's population live in circumstances of relative squalor when it has been demonstrated that the principles of the market and free enterprise can lead to sustained economic development?*"(italics in orginal).

This is not to suggest that positive psychology, or positive anything, is part of a right-wing conspiracy. Pop positive thinking has a mixed political lineage: Norman Vincent Peale was an outspoken conservative, at least until his attacks on a Catholic candidate, John F. Kennedy, resulted in charges of bigotry. On the other hand, perhaps the most famous contemporary promoter of positive thinking is Oprah Winfrey, whom we normally think of as a liberal. As for positive psychology, Seligman himself certainly leans to the right. He is famously impatient with "victims" and "victimology," saying, for example, in a 2000 interview: "In general when things go wrong we now have a culture which supports the belief that this was done to you by some larger force, as opposed to, you brought it on yourself by your character or your decisions."[44] It also turns out that he has spoken about his "learned helplessness" experiments with dogs at one of the military's SERE (Survival, Evasion, Resistance, Escape) schools, which were originally designed to help U.S. troops survive capture but changed their mission, post-9/11, to devising new forms of torture for suspected terrorists.[45] (Seligman denies he was contributing to torture, writing in a 2008 e-mail that "I strongly disapprove of torture and have never and would never provide assistance in its process.") As for rank-and-file positive psychologists, a rising star in the positive psychology firmament, Jonathan Haidt of the University of Virginia, insisted to me that most positive psychologists are probably liberal in their personal outlooks. Certainly many of them see themselves as rebels against a hidebound establishment of psychologists still obsessed with "negative" subjects such as depression, neurosis, and suffering.

But positive psychology seems to have exhausted its rebellious spirit in the battle against "negative psychology" and today offers much to warm the most conservative hearts, including its finding that married and highly religious people—preferably fundamentalists—are happier than other people, as are political conservatives.[46] Happiness, after all, is generally measured as reported satisfaction with one's life—a state of mind perhaps more accessible to those who are affluent, who conform to social norms, who suppress judgment in the service of faith, and who are not overly bothered by societal injustice. Strangely though, the arrival of children—which one would expect to result from fundamentalist marriages—actually decreases the happiness of the parents, and, according to Harvard psychologist Daniel Gilbert, "the only known symptom of 'empty nest syndrome' is increased smiling."[47]

The real conservativism of positive psychology lies in its attachment to the status quo, with all its inequalities and abuses of power. Positive psychologists' tests of happiness and well-being, for example, rest heavily on measures of personal contentment with things as they are. Consider the widely used "Satisfaction with Life Scale" developed by Diener and others, which asks the respondent to agree or disagree with the following propositions:

> In most ways my life is close to my ideal.
> The conditions of my life are excellent.
> I am satisfied with my life.
> So far I have gotten the important things I want in life.
> If I could live my life over, I would change almost nothing.[48]

One could imagine positive psychology, or a more liberal version thereof, spawning a movement to alter social arrangements in the direction of greater happiness—by advocating more democratically organized workplaces, to suggest just one example. Instead, positive psychology seems to have weighed in on the side of the employers, with Seligman collaborator Chris Peterson telling the *Cleveland Plain Dealer* in 2008 that business executives are particularly enthused about the new happiness science: "Hard-headed corporate culture is becoming interested in how to get more work out of fewer workers. They're realizing that if their workers are happy, they will work harder and more productively. So they're leading the charge."[49] As for social action against societal injustice, the American Psychological Association's *Monitor* reported in 1998: "Seligman asserts that . . . those who reproach others and side with the underdog may feel better in the short term, . . . but such good feelings are transient."[50] Why social activism should produce only fleeting good feelings—compared with performing other virtuous deeds, viewing Monets, or reading Richard Russo—is not explained.

Like pop positive thinking, positive psychology attends almost solely to the changes a person can make internally by adjusting his or her own outlook. Seligman himself explicitly rejects social change, writing of the role of "circumstances" in determining human happiness: "The good news about circumstances is that some do change happiness for the better. The bad news is that changing these circumstances is usually impractical and expensive."[51] This argument—"impractical and expensive"—has of course been used against almost every progressive reform from the abolition of slavery to pay equity for women.

Positive psychologists' more important contribution to the defense of the status quo has been to assert or "find" that circumstances play only a minor role in determining a person's happiness. In their misbegotten equation—$H = S + C + V$—"C," for circumstances, is generally judged to make a small contribution to the total, only around 8 to 15 percent.[52] A variety of studies are usually cited in support of the inconsequence of C, finding, for example, that people who lose their jobs or who are rendered paraplegic by severe spinal-cord injuries quickly revert to their original levels of happiness. When I interviewed Seligman, he said that new evidence shows that paraplegics and the unemployed "do not go back to where they were," and he estimated that C could be as high as 25 percent, adding that "there is a lot of controversy over the size of C, since it brings up the question of whether policy matters."

Indeed, if circumstances play only a small role—even 25 percent—in human happiness, then policy is a marginal exercise.

Why advocate for better jobs and schools, safer neighborhoods, universal health insurance, or any other liberal desideratum if these measures will do little to make people happy? Social reformers, political activists, and change-oriented elected officials can all take a much-needed rest. And since no one is talking about using gene therapy to raise "S," a person's happiness "set point," that leaves only "V," one's voluntary efforts, to tinker with. In the great centuries-long quest for a better world, the baton has passed to the practitioners of "optimism training," the positive psychologists, and the purveyors of pop positive thinking.

The next time I met Martin Seligman he was unexpectedly friendly and welcoming. The setting was the Sixth International Positive Psychology Summit, held in the majestic Gallup Organization building in downtown D.C. He invited me to sit down next to him and asked whether I had enjoyed the morning session's "energy break." This had been a five-minute interval embedded in a presentation on teaching positive psychology at the graduate level, led by some female graduate students. The audience was instructed to stand, do a few shoulder rolls and neck stretches, shake their bodies, and then utter a big collective "Aaaah." When we were loosened up, we were treated to the pounding beat of Ricky Martin's "Cup of Life," and the women on stage began to dance along in an awkward, choreographed way, while some in the audience boogied freestyle and a few of the older men stamped around as if putting out fires. I told Seligman I had liked the energy break well enough, not bothering to mention how closely it resembled the audience exercises undertaken by motivational speakers at the National Speakers Association.

At the time of the "summit" meeting, in October 2007, positive psychology had a lot to celebrate. It was gaining ground at all levels in academia, with more than two hundred colleges and graduate schools offering courses in positive psychology, sometimes dubbed "Happiness 101," in which students reflected on their happier moments and engaged in exercises like writing "gratitude letters" to people in their lives. At Harvard, the introductory positive psychology course had drawn 855 students in 2006, making it the most popular course on campus, surpassing even economics, and a similar undergraduate course at George Mason University was the subject of a *New York Times Magazine* article in early 2007.[53] Graduate-level courses, like those required for the master of applied positive psychology degree at the University of Pennsylvania, were popping up all over the world. According to one summit speaker, Ilona Boniwell of the University of East London, "rapid growth" of postgrad programs could be expected in Argentina, Australia, India, Israel, Mexico, Spain, and Singapore.

Moreover, attractive careers seemed to await those who earned higher degrees in positive psychology. The University of Pennsylvania program claims as one of its alums a coauthor of the business self-help book *How Full Is Your Bucket?* and two other alums have founded a consulting group to bring positive psychology into the public schools, through workshops on such topics as "measuring and nurturing character strengths and virtues" and "learning tools for building optimism and resilience."[54] Another alum, David J. Pollay, is a business consultant and columnist for the Happy News Web site. Mostly, the opportunities seemed to lie in applying positive psychology to organizations and businesses, through consulting and coaching. In a breakout session so packed that many attendees had to sit on the floor, a British consultant who said that he helps clients like Wells Fargo and Microsoft create "strength-based organizations" offered a PowerPoint presentation listing the terms "natural and authentic," "energizing," "engaging," "learning and developing," "high performing," and "well-being and fulfillment." Similar lists, maddeningly nonparallel combinations of adjectives and nouns, pass for "theory" in most pop positive-thinking books directed at business audiences, making me wonder what distinguishes an academically trained positive psychology coach from the thousands of self-appointed coaches and motivators who feed off the business world.

Yet even at this self-congratulatory "summit," there was some anxiety about the scientific foundations of positive psychology. In her description of the "challenges" facing the master's program in positive psychology at her London university, Ilona Boniwell had included "healthy British skepticism." This struck me as odd: Wouldn't a physics or sociology professor be delighted to have skeptical, questioning students? When I put this query to her during a break in the proceedings, she told me: "A lot of results [in positive psychology] are presented as stronger than they are; for example, they're correlational, not causative. The science of positive psychology has not necessarily caught up with the promise of positive psychology." The "promise" was lucrative careers in business coaching, and the science would apparently just have to catch up.

In fact, the publicity received by positive psychology in the preceding year had been less than 100 percent positive. The 2007 *New York Times Magazine* article on Happiness 101 courses had complained about "the sect-like feel of positive psychology" and suggested that "the publicity about the field has gotten ahead of the science, which may be no good anyway." The article went on to report that "the idea that whatever science there is may not yet be first-class troubles Seligman, too. 'I have the same worry they do. That's what I do at 4 in the morning,' he says."[55]

These worries finally surfaced at a late afternoon plenary session on "The Future of Positive Psychology," featuring the patriarchs of the discipline, Martin Seligman and Ed Diener. Seligman got the audience's attention by starting off with the statement "I've decided my theory of positive psychology is completely wrong." Why? Because it's about happiness, which is "scientifically unwieldy." Somehow, this problem could be corrected by throwing in the notions of "success" and "accomplishment"—which I couldn't help noting would put the positive psychologists on the same terrain as Norman Vincent Peale and any number of success gurus. With the addition of success, Seligman went on, one was talking no longer about positive *psychology* but about a "plural theory" embracing anthropology, political science, and economics, and this is what he would be moving on to—"positive social science."

Seligman's statement created understandable consternation within the audience of several hundred positive psychologists, graduate students, and coaches. It must have felt a bit like having one's father announce that he found his current family too narrow and limiting and would be moving on to a new one. In the Q&A session, some picked up on Seligman's admission that the scientific basis of positive psychology is all too thin, with one asking, "How do we balance the empirical side of positive psychology with the applied stuff," like coaching? Diener responded, in part, that "people doing things that there isn't good evidence for" are at least "meeting a need." Seligman agreed, saying that positive psychology was under pressure to produce practical results because "people want happiness." If that sometimes means that the applications, like coaching, get ahead of the science—well, "science follows from practice," he said, invoking the Wright brothers, "who flew when scientists didn't know how birds fly."

The idea of moving on to "positive social science" provoked even more anxiety. Diener defended the phrase "positive psychology," saying, "It's a brand." Besides, he said, he "hates" the idea of positive social science, since social science includes sociology and sociology is "weak" and notoriously underfunded. The subject seemed to have veered away from science to naked opportunism. When one audience member proposed renaming positive psychology "applied behavioral economics," because "it's popular in business schools and goes with high salaries," nobody laughed.

SEVEN

How Positive Thinking
Destroyed the Economy

In the middle of the first decade of the twenty-first century, positive thoughts were flowing out into the universe in unprecedented volumes, escaping the solar system, rippling through vast bodies of interstellar gas, dodging black holes, messing with the tides of distant planets. If anyone—deity or alien being—possessed the means of transforming these emanations into comprehensible form, they would have been overwhelmed by images of slimmer bodies, larger homes, quick promotions, and sudden acquisitions of great wealth.

But the universe refused to play its assigned role as a "big mail order department." In complete defiance of the "law of attraction," long propounded by the gurus of positive thinking, things were getting worse for most Americans, not better. The poor, including those who sought spiritual leadership from prosperity preachers like Joel Osteen and Creflo Dollar, remained poor and even increased in numbers. Between 2002 and 2006, as the economy grew briskly, the number of officially "low-wage" families shot up to 25 percent of all families with children.[1] The traditional working class, which had once overlapped with the middle class, saw its wages decline and decent-paying jobs—in manufacturing, for example—disappear. For many, the operative word seemed to be "squeezed," as illustrated by books like Jared Bernstein's *Crunch: Why Do I Feel So Squeezed?* and Steven Greenhouse's *The Big Squeeze: Tough Times for the American Worker*.

The white-collar middle class—prime market for self-help books, motivational products, and coaching services—found itself subject to the same forces of compression. Companies were cutting back or eliminating employee pensions and health benefits, a trend documented by Jacob Hacker in *The Great Risk Shift: The Assault on American Jobs, Families, Health Care, and Retirement*. Unemployment was low in the middle of the decade, but jobs were becoming increasingly short-lived as employers downsized, reorganized, outsourced, and otherwise sought to tweak their quarterly profits. In *High Wire: The Precarious Financial Lives of American Families*, Peter Gosselin described how the once-secure middle class was now being tossed about by "income volatility"— sudden downturns occasioned by layoffs, leaving families without health insurance or the means to continue their home payments. I reported on this stomach-churning situation in a 2006 book, *Bait and Switch: On the (Futile) Pursuit of the American Dream*, finding educated and experienced white-collar workers adrift in joblessness and short-term contract jobs and likely to end up in the same low-wage service jobs occupied by the chronically poor.

Not everyone was seeing their prospects diminish and lifestyle crimped. The flip side of all this poverty and insecurity was an unimaginably huge buildup of wealth at the upper extreme of the economic spectrum. In terms of wealth and income, America became the most polarized of the First World societies and even more deeply divided than it had been in the 1920s. The share of pretax income going to the top 1 percent of American households rose by 7 percentage points from 1979 to 2007, to 16 percent, while the share of income going to the bottom 80 percent fell by 7 percentage points. As David Leonhardt put it in the *New York Times*: "It's as if every household in that bottom 80 percent is writing a check for $7,000 every year and sending it to the top 1 percent."[2] How did the top 1 percent use their ballooning wealth? On high-yield investments, of course, but also on a level of consumption that might have stunned even the robber barons of old. They traveled by Lear jet, maintained multiple homes, and hired whole staffs of personal employees, including people whose job it was to advise them on the best wines and art to invest in. Looking back from 2008, a writer in the business magazine *Portfolio* marveled at

> the $34,000-a-night hotel rooms, the $175 gold-dusted Richard Nouveau hamburger at the Wall Street Burger Shoppe, the Algonquin Hotel's $10,000 martini on the rock (the rock in question: a jeweler-selected diamond): Conspicuous consumption didn't even begin to describe the you're-not-going-to-believe-this lifestyle and work habits of the rapacious übercapitalists who were replicating all over the world.[3]

On the eve of the Great Depression, in the highly polarized 1920s, there had been plenty of labor organizers and radical activists around to rail about the excesses of the rich and the misery of the poor. In the twenty-first century, a very different and more numerous breed of ideologues promulgated the opposite message—that all was well with our deeply unequal society and, for those willing to make the effort, about to get much, much better. The motivators and other purveyors of positive thinking had good news for people facing economic ruin from the constant churning of the job market: embrace "change," no matter how terrifying; grasp it as an opportunity. A 2004 business self-help book by Harvey Mackay bore the defiant title *We Got Fired! . . . And It's the Best Thing That Ever Happened to Us*. As we saw in chapter 4, employers relied on positive thinking to soothe the victims of downsizings and extract ever more heroic efforts from the survivors.

Nor was economic inequality a concern to positive thinkers, since anyone, anyone at all, could be catapulted into wealth at any time simply by focusing their thoughts. In the 2008 presidential campaign, Joe Wurzelbach, an Ohio man nicknamed "Joe the Plumber," achieved a moment of fame for challenging Barack Obama's plan to raise taxes for people earning over $250,000 a year. He was planning to buy the plumbing business he worked for, he asserted, and would soon be in that enviable category himself. As it turned out, he was an unlicensed plumber working in a two-man residential business that was unlikely to ever be vulnerable to the proposed tax increase. But why resent the swelling overclass—the CEOs earning an average of $11 million a year, the owners of islands and yachts—when you are aiming to join their ranks? In reality, Americans are less likely to move upward from their class of origin than are Germans, Canadians, Finns, French people, Swedes, Norwegians, or Danes.[4] But the myth, fortified with bracing doses of positive thinking, persists. As two researchers at the Brookings Institution observed, a little wryly, in 2006: "[The] strong belief in opportunity and upward mobility is the explanation that is often given for Americans' high tolerance for inequality. The majority of Americans surveyed believe that they will be above mean income in the future (even though that is a mathematical impossibility)."[5]

Hardly anyone—economist or otherwise—predicted the financial meltdown. After all, the American economy had recovered handily from the traumas of the dot-com bust and 9/11 and was being carried to new heights by soaring housing and stock prices. Professional optimists dominated the world of economic commentary, with James Glassman, for example, a coauthor of the 1999 book *Dow 36,000: The New Strategy for Profiting from the Coming Rise in the Stock Market*, winning a job as a *Washington Post* columnist and showing up as a frequent news show guest. Escalating housing prices were pumping up the entire economy by encouraging people to use their homes "like ATMs," as the commentators always put it—taking out home equity loans to finance surging consumption—and housing prices were believed to be permanently resistant to gravity. David Lereah, the chief economist of the National Association of Realtors, published a book in 2006 entitled *Why the Real Estate Boom Will Not Bust and How You Can Profit from It* and became "the most widely cited housing expert in major media outlets during the peak years of the housing bubble."[6] Frank Nothaft, the chief economist at Freddie Mac, was assuring audiences that nationwide housing prices would never fall significantly. Late in 2008, one of the rare economic pessimists, *New York Times* columnist Paul Krugman, asked rhetorically why no one had seen that "the whole thing was, in effect, a giant Ponzi scheme" and offered, as an answer, "that nobody likes to be a party pooper."[7]

The near unanimous optimism of the experts certainly contributed to the reckless buildup of bad debt and dodgy loans, but so did the wildly upbeat outlook of many ordinary Americans. Robert Reich once observed, a bit ambivalently, that "American optimism carries over into our economy, which is one reason why we've always been a nation of inventors and tinkerers, of innovators and experimenters. . . . Optimism also explains why we spend so much and save so little. . . . Our willingness to go deep into debt and keep spending is intimately related to our optimism."[8]

It's in the spirit of optimism that a person blithely builds up credit card debt on optional expenditures, takes out a second mortgage, or agrees to a mortgage with an interest rate that will escalate over time. And the ideology of positive thinking eagerly fanned this optimism and the sense of entitlement that went with it. A *Los Angeles Times* reporter wrote of the effect of *The Secret* on her sister: "When my sister arrived from New York over the holidays, she plopped a hand-tooled leather satchel on my piano bench and said, 'See the beautiful bag I manifested for myself?'" The DVD of *The Secret* had encouraged her to believe that she deserved this object, that it was hers for the taking, so she had charged it on her Amex card.[9]

While secular positive-thinking texts encouraged people to "manifest" their material desires, pastors like Osteen and Dollar were insisting that God *wants* you to have the all good things in life, including a beautiful home. In *Your Best Life Now,* Joel Osteen had written about his initial resistance to his wife's pleadings that they upgrade to a large and "elegant" house: "Over the next several months, she kept speaking words of faith and victory, and she finally talked me into it. . . . I don't believe it would have happened if Victoria had not talked me into enlarging my vision. God has so much more in store for you, too."[10] A 2008 article in *Time*, provocatively titled "Maybe We Should Blame God for the Subprime Mortgage Mess," cited the suspicions of several experts on American religion about the role of prosperity preachers in fomenting the financial meltdown. Jonathan Walton, a religion professor at the University of California at Riverside, argued that pastors like Osteen reassured low-income people with subprime mortgages by getting them to believe that "God caused the bank to ignore my credit score and bless me with my first house." Anthea Butler, an expert on Pentecostalism, added: "The pastor's not gonna say, 'Go down to Wachovia and get a loan,' but I have heard, 'Even if you have a poor credit rating, God can still bless you—if you put some faith out there [that is, make a big donation to the church], you'll get that house or that car or that apartment.'"[11] To Kevin Phillips, the connection between positive thinking and the subprime crisis seems obvious. In *Bad Money: Reckless Finance, Failed Politics, and the Global Crisis of American Capitalism*, he indicts prosperity preachers Osteen, T. D. Jakes, and Creflo Dollar, along with *The Secret* author Rhonda Byrne.[12]

To many people who had long been denied credit on account of their race or income, the easy mortgages of the middle of the decade must have indeed come as a miracle from God. Dean Baker, one of the few economists who foresaw the bursting of the housing bubble, reports that in 2006 the dicey subprime and Alt-A categories of mortgages had expanded to 40 percent of total mortgages— many of them requiring little or no income documentation or down payment.[13] No wonder that within a year more and more Americans were finding themselves in over their heads. Household debt hit a record 133 percent of household income, for an absolute amount of about $14 trillion.[14] Personal bankruptcy filings jumped by 40 percent in the course of 2007 alone.[15] People who were unprepared for their adjustable mortgages' rate increases started defaulting, often moving out in the dead of night to avoid their neighbors' stares.

But the gullibility and optimism of ordinary individuals go only so far in explaining the financial crisis. *Someone* was offering tricky mortgages to people of dubious means, someone was bundling up those mortgage debts and selling them as securities to investors throughout the world—someone who was expecting to make sizable profits by doing so. As *Washington Post* columnist Steven Pearlstein has written: "At the heart of any economic or financial mania is an epidemic of self-delusion that infects not only large numbers of unsophisticated investors but also many of the smartest, most experienced and sophisticated executives and bankers."[16] In fact, the recklessness of the borrowers was far exceeded by that of the lenders, with some finance companies involved in subprimes undertaking debt-to-asset ratios of 30 to 1.[17] Recall that American corporate culture had long since abandoned the dreary rationality of professional management for the emotional thrills of mysticism, charisma, and sudden intuitions. Pumped up by paid motivators and divinely inspired CEOs, American business entered the midyears of the decade at a manic peak of delusional expectations, extending to the highest levels of leadership.

One exemplar of the fashionable nonrational approach to management was Joe Gregory, former president of the former investment company Lehman Brothers. According to a 2008 article in *New York* magazine, Gregory was known as a "warm and fuzzy" person, a good golf companion, and, as Gregory himself put it, a "Feeler" with a capital F. Not for him the tedium of detailed risk analysis. "He was Mr. Instinct," in the words of another Lehman executive. "Trusting your instincts, trusting your judgment, believing in yourself . . . and making decisions on the back of that trust is a remarkably powerful thing," Gregory had said in a speech to one group, even when that instinct contradicted rational analysis. Sometimes, Gregory's hunches would lead Lehman to "decide that we should be doing the exact opposite of what the analysis said," according to one analyst.[18]

In April 2008, I interviewed one of the few dissenters from the prevailing positive-thinking consensus. Eric Dezenhall is a Washington, D.C., "crisis manager"—someone companies call in when faced with a potential public relations disaster. A short, blunt, intense man with an impeccable Republican background (he was an intern in the Reagan administration), Dezenhall has often found himself at odds with his own clients: "A lot of corporate types don't want to hear what I have to tell them." In fact, he said, it can be a "career ender" to be the bearer of bad news. However dire the situation, "corporate America desperately wants to believe there's a positive outcome and message." When called in by companies to deal with a crisis, he starts by telling them, "I'm going to tell you something you're not going to like: 'A crisis is *not* an opportunity.'" I asked him whether he thought corporate decision makers went so far as to embrace the "law of attraction," or the idea that you can control the world with your thoughts, and he replied that this way of thinking was "viral" in corporate America. "They believe this stuff. Corporations can be ruthless about making money, but when it comes to being realistic . . ."

The once sober finance sector was not immune to the "virus" of positive thinking. Finance companies hired motivational speakers and coaches like Tony Robbins, who boasted to Larry King in 2008 that he'd "had the privilege of coaching one of the top 10 financial traders in the world for 16 years" and was currently consulting to a group of traders including "the smartest minds around."[19] Some finance companies even generated their own motivational speakers. Chris Gardner, for example, whose account of his rise from homelessness to a top-earning position at Bear Stearns—*The Pursuit of Happyness*—became a best seller and a Hollywood movie, is a popular motivational speaker. Another motivational speaker, Chuck Mills, spent several years with Bear Stearns as a trader for a $300 million portfolio before going on to found his own financial services firm and speaking business. So profound was the optimism of the finance sector that, when the crisis hit in 2008, Merrill Lynch suddenly found itself having to "temper the Pollyannas in its ranks" and force its analysts to occasionally say the word "sell."[20]

Or consider the somewhat tipsy case of Countrywide Mortgage, the company whose rash lending practices almost singlehandedly set off the subprime crisis that preceded the global credit melt-down. In 2004, Countrywide's CEO, Angelo Mozilo, ever smiling through his bright orange tan, had been the recipient of the Hora-tio Alger Award as "an individual who has emerged from humble beginnings to prove that hard work, determination and positive thinking are key to successfully achieving the American dream."[21] Even as his company's stock plummeted in early 2008, the press consistently found him "optimistic" and "upbeat." Bruce C. N. Greenwald, a finance professor at Columbia Business School, said of Mozilo: "People who get themselves in trouble are good at self-hypnosis. That is why they are such good salesmen—they con-vince themselves about the story. . . . And he had lived in a world where there had been no defaults for so long that he didn't believe they could happen."[22]

The same happy conviction prevailed throughout the company during its years of glad-handed lending. In a tell-all book about his time as a senior vice president at Countrywide, Adam Michaelson describes the "marginally cultish behavior" at the company, char-acterized by what he calls a "woo" culture of high fives, motivational speakers, and loud "woo" cheers. When, in 2004, he questioned the assumption of ever-rising housing prices, he was told, "You know what? You worry too much." Even as the subprime mortgage mar-ket imploded, he writes, the woo culture prevailed: "These are the times when that one person who might respond with a negative comment or a cautious appraisal might be the first to be ostra-cized. There is a great risk in noncomformity in any feverishly frothy environment like that."[23] Interestingly, among the motiva-tional speakers I could find listing Countrywide as a client was Buford P. Fuddwhacker (actually the fictional alter ego of the real motivational speaker Roger Reece), who is described as "a down-home motivational speaker who brings the fervor and energy of a fired-up country preacher to the platform. When you unleash Buford on your audience, get ready for music, laughter, kazoos, kara-oke, and outrageous audience participation."

In a remarkable essay entitled "The End of Wall Street's Boom," business writer Michael Lewis provides a glimpse into how positive thinking turned toxic on Wall Street. He set out to find insiders who had anticipated the disaster, and, not surprisingly, some of the people he found had been under pressure over the years to improve their attitude. Ivy Zelman, an analyst at Credit Suisse who foresaw the bursting of the housing bubble, "alienated clients with her pessimism, but she couldn't pretend everything was good." Another analyst, banking expert Steve Eisman, faced criticism for putting a "sell" rating on a company because, as Lewis quotes him, "it was a piece of shit. I didn't know that you weren't supposed to put a sell rating on companies. I thought there were three boxes—buy, hold, sell—and you picked the one you thought you should." He was, in other words, a holdover from a more rational approach to business, when the job of midlevel people was not just to soothe or flatter the men at the top. Lewis relates that Eisman "was pressured generally to be a bit more upbeat, but upbeat wasn't Steve Eisman's style. Upbeat and Eisman didn't occupy the same planet."[24] When I talked to Eisman by phone a couple of weeks after Lewis's article came out, he said the finance industry had "built assumption on top of assumption"—such as that housing prices would never fall—and that "no one saw any reason to question those assumptions." There was a good reason to remain silent about the enveloping madness, he told me: "Anybody who voiced negativity was thrown out."

One such martyr to the cause of financial realism was Mike Gelband, who was Global Head of Fixed Income at Lehman Brothers. At the end of 2006, Gelband was getting nervous about what looked increasingly like a real estate bubble. "The world is changing," Gelband told Lehman CEO Richard Fuld during his 2006

bonus review. "We have to rethink our business model." Fuld
promptly fired the misfit and, two years later, Lehman went bank-
rupt. *New York* magazine reports that, as of late 2008, Fuld still
had not absorbed what Gelband was trying to tell him:

> At night, Fuld has trouble sleeping. Most of the time,
> he lives in Greenwich, Connecticut, in one of his five
> houses. He can wander through the twenty rooms,
> eight bedrooms, the poolhouse, tennis court, squash
> court. Mostly, he sits and replays Lehman's calami-
> tous end. "What could I have done differently?" he
> thinks. . . . How, he wonders, did it all go so disas-
> trously wrong?[25]

Or we might cite the case of Armando Falcon, a government
official charged with oversight of Fannie Mae and Freddie Mac.
When he issued a report in 2003 warning that the two mortgage
giants were in parlous financial condition that could result in
"contagious illiquidity in the market"—that is, a general financial
meltdown—the White House tried to fire him.[26]

It's almost impossible to trace the attitudes of failed titans like
Fuld to particular ideologues of positive thinking—the coaches
and motivators who advise, for example, that one purge "negative
people" from the ranks. Among top executives, there's a degree of
secretiveness about the use of coaches. In the UK, for example, an
estimated one-third of CEOs of FTSE 100 companies used personal coaches in 2007, but as a writer in the *Spectator* commented,
"Consulting a coach is still regarded by senior businesspeople as
private and absolutely not something to declare openly."[27] More
likely, though, a top guy like Fuld didn't need anyone whispering
in his ear that he could have anything he wanted, if only he con-
centrated on it hard enough. At $60 million a year—his average

compensation between 2000 and 2008—this was already his reality, without his even having to concentrate.

Corporate leaders, in the finance sector and elsewhere, had ascended into a shimmering bubble of wealth floating miles above the anxieties and cares of everyone else. Between 1965 and 2000, the ratio of CEO pay to that of a typical worker soared from 24:1 to 300:1, and the gap also widened between the CEO and his or her third in command.[28] Robert Frank documented the fabulous wealth at the top in his book *Richistan: A Journey through the American Wealth Boom and the Lives of the New Rich*. If, for example, you were in your Palm Beach home and found that you'd left the Château Latour in your Southampton wine cellar, a private jet could be dispatched to fetch it.[29] Take the case of Jack Welch, whom we last saw in chapter 4, mowing down middle-class jobs. He retired from GE with a monthly income of $2.1 million, as well as the use of a company-provided Boeing 737 and an $80,000-a-month Manhattan apartment, in addition to free security guards for his various homes.[30] On one postretirement trip to London, the *Independent* found him "installed in the suite of suites in the Lanesborough Hotel overlooking Hyde Park. Dark-suited flunkies with little GE lapel pins stand around looking menacing. One or two have earpieces and curly wires going back down their necks, like G-men protecting the President."[31]

One obvious price of this lifestyle is extreme isolation—what Dezenhall calls "bubble-itis." Subordinates suffer from "the galloping desire to bring good news" rather than honest reports, leading one billionaire CEO to complain to Dezenhall that "I'm the most lied-to man in the world." Dezenhall can't offer examples from among his own clients, of course, but he points to the film *Michael Clayton*, in which Tilda Swinton's character arranges to have a whistle-blower murdered rather than confront her boss with the

developing mess. Again, the defunct Lehman Brothers provides a
case study. According to *New York*, by the summer of 2008:

> There was a disconnect to the outside world, and the
> risk was substantial. "The environment had become
> so insular," said one former executive. Fuld okayed
> decisions, but [Joe] Gregory packaged material so that
> the choice was obvious. And the executive committee
> offered no counterweight.... In truth, the relentless
> optimism, both inside and out [of the company], was
> probably doing as much harm as good.[32]

Then there is the effect of being walled inside a world of unstint-
ing luxury. Fuld had his five homes; Gregory commuted to work
by helicopter from one of his "sprawling Long Island homes."[33]
"The problem with this," Dezenhall and his coauthor write in a
book on crisis management, "is that when a subject goes from a
Gulfstream V airplane to a limousine to a catered meeting to a four-
star hotel, he lives in an artificial bubble of constant, uncritical
reinforcement. He becomes a demigod who is a consumer of reas-
suring clichés, not of life's friction."[34] And of course one thing
that would be invisible from 30,000 feet up in a Gulfstream jet
was the kind of everyday emergency that was derailing so many
mortgage holders—a child's illness leading to medical bills and
days lost from work, a costly car breakdown, a surprise layoff.

Steve Eisman is far harsher about the executive mind-set that
led to the market crack-up. He calls it "hedge fund disease" and
says "it should be in the DSM-V [the latest manual of psychiatric
disorders, currently in preparation]. It used to be suffered only by
kings and dictators. The symptoms are megalomania, plus narcis-
sism, plus solipsism." If you're worth $500 million, he asks, "how

could you be wrong about anything? To think something is to make it happen. You're God." This is the state of mind promoted by every positive thinker from Mary Baker Eddy to Joel Osteen, from Norman Vincent Peale to Rhonda Byrne. Corporate chiefs had, perhaps somewhat cynically, long recommended it to their underlings. They had distributed motivational books and brought in motivational speakers to inspire people to visualize success, to work harder and complain less. The problem is that they came to believe it themselves, with the eventual result that, in a short period of time, about $3 trillion worth of pension funds, retirement accounts, and life savings evaporated into the same ether that had absorbed all our positive thoughts.

"Where were the grown-ups?" asked the commentators as the economy unraveled in 2008. Where were the regulators, the watchdogs, the rating agencies, like Moody's, that were supposed to make careful assessments of investment risks? Well, the rating agencies, as we have learned, were in the pocket of the very companies they were supposed to be judging—were even paid by them, perversely enough.[35] As for the public and quasi-public sector, it was in the grip of its own optimistic faith—market fundamentalism, or the idea that markets are self-correcting and in no need of burdensome regulation. One true believer was Alan Greenspan, chairman of the Federal Reserve until 2006, who had crowed in 2005 that "the impressive performance of the U.S. economy over the past couple of decades offers clear evidence of the benefits of increased market flexibility," with "flexibility" meaning freedom from regulation and burdensome trade unions. Three years later he was eating crow, famously admitting to a congressional committee that "those of us who have looked to the self-interest of lending institutions to protect shareholders' equity are in a state of shocked disbelief."[36]

And what was market fundamentalism other than runaway positive thinking? In the ideology that prevailed in the Bush administration and, to a somewhat lesser extent, the Clinton administration before it, there was no need for vigilance or anxiety about America's financial institutions, because "the market" would take care of everything. It achieved the status of a deity, this market, closely related to Mary Baker Eddy's benevolent, ever-nurturing, and all-supplying universe. Why worry, when Adam Smith's "invisible hand" would straighten everything out?

The purveyors of positive thinking did not slink off into the night like foreclosed-upon homeowners when the prospects for instant wealth tanked in the late years of the decade. Not at all. In fact, they seemed to redouble their efforts. Positive thinking has always thrived in adversity, with the Great Depression bringing forth such classics of self-delusion as Napoleon Hill's *Think and Grow Rich!* In late 2008, as the financial meltdown touched off general economic decline and widespread unemployment, as the commentators increasingly questioned the durability of capitalism itself, attendance was soaring at evangelical churches, including those offering the prosperity gospel.[37] Joel and Victoria Osteen took to the national media with their message of victory and faith, telling Larry King that their advice to people who had lost their jobs, their homes, and their health insurance was to avoid seeing themselves "as victims": "You've got to know that God still has a plan and that even if you lost your job, even if one door closes, God can open up another door." A new series of "Get Motivated!" seminars was announced, featuring Rudolph Giuliani, Robert Schuller, and veteran motivator Zig Ziglar. A speakers agency reported that requests from mortgage companies for motivational speakers rose 20 percent as the mortgage industry declined in 2007.[38]

Employers turned to the motivation industry for the usual

reason—to maintain discipline within a demoralized workforce. The pharmaceutical company Novo Nordisk, for example, bought up seven hundred "Positive Power" CDs from motivational speaker Ed Blunt, hoping they would serve as "a catalyst for employee productivity."[39] A late November 2008 conference on "Happiness and Its Causes" attracted, among hundreds of others, a senior vice president of a large mortgage company. As the *New York Times* reported, she said that "she had laid off more than 500 people in the last six months, and was there to learn how to boost the morale of employees working weekends and holidays and making do with bonuses cut in half, . . . adding that companies like hers were not totally at fault for the mortgage crisis."[40] The message to downcast employees could be fluffily optimistic, like Osteen's, or downright harsh, like that of the motivational speaker who told a St. Petersburg, Florida, business conference that when people write to her saying "they can't pretend to be upbeat at work when they feel so miserable," she tells them to "fake it." As for workplace "change," generally meaning layoffs, her advice is, "Deal with it, you big babies."[41]

With real jobs disappearing, the positive thinkers counseled people to work ever harder on themselves—monitoring their thoughts, adjusting their emotions, focusing more intently on their desires. All the usual nostrums were invoked: Banish negative people and steer clear of "office water-cooler whinefests."[42] Limit your consumption of negative news. Even on the liberal news site the *Huffington Post*, a blogger advised, "Studies show that you will sleep better with less news intake late at night. Focus your mind on what is upbeat and positive."[43] Above all, it was important to be vigilant and learn how "to spot when negativity is sneaking up on you personally," according to an advertisement for a positive-thinking seminar directed both at managers and at "individuals who are experiencing a personal loss of drive and feeling of futility."

Bear in mind that even in the worst catastrophe someone usually comes out on top, Tony Robbins assured viewers of the *Today* show, citing Sir John Templeton, "the greatest investor of all time," who "made most of his money when markets were crashing."[44] If just one person can get rich during a crash or economic downturn, then no one has an excuse for whining.

Some recommended positive thinking as a cure not only for the individual's plight but for the entire economic mess. What is a recession, anyway, but a mass outbreak of pessimism? An op-ed in the *Chicago Tribune* asserted that "the constant bad-mouthing, beyond what reality requires, got us to where we are now, turning a limp economy into a poor one, threatening to turn a recession into a depression." The solution? "Knock off the bad-mouthing. Brush off the accusations of being Pollyannaish, naive, or worse. . . . Exult in the prospects, understand that we can pour whatever trillions we can get our hands on into the economy, but it won't do any good unless we, ourselves, look forward with trust and confidence."[45] Similarly, the broker who handles my dwindling retirement account suggested wistfully that "if only people would get out and buy things again . . ." But at the time of this writing, Adam Smith's idea that the self-seeking behavior of individuals would add up to the general welfare of all no longer seems to apply. As individuals, we know that it would be suicidal to get deeper in debt to indulge our acquisitiveness, even if doing so could jump-start the economy, so we each hunker down and try to make do with less. The easy credit is gone; the reckless spending looks more self-destructive by the moment. Besides, we already tried all that.

EIGHT

Postscript on Post–Positive Thinking

What can we be if not positive? "I do believe in the power of positive thinking," veteran newspaper editor Ben Bradlee wrote recently. "I don't know any other way to live."[1] We've gone so far down this yellow brick road that "positive" seems to us not only normal but normative—the way you *should* be. A restaurant not far from where I live calls itself the "Positive Pizza and Pasta Place," apparently distinguishing itself from the many sullen and negative Italian dining options. A veteran human resources executive, baffled by my questions about positive thinking in the workplace, ventured hesitantly, "But isn't positive . . . *good*?" He was right: we have come to use the words "positive" and "good" almost interchangeably. In this moral system, either you look on the bright side, constantly adjusting your attitude and revising your perceptions—or you go over to the dark side.

The alternative to positive thinking is not, however, despair. In fact, negative thinking can be just as delusional as the positive

kind. Depressed people project their misery onto the world, imagining worst outcomes from every endeavor and then feeding their
misery on these distorted expectations. In both cases, there is an
inability to separate emotion from perception, a willingness to
accept illusion for reality, either because it "feels good" or, in the
depressive's case, because it reinforces familiar, downwardly spiraling neural pathways. The alternative to both is to try to get
outside of ourselves and see things "as they are," or as uncolored as
possible by our own feelings and fantasies, to understand that the
world is full of both danger and opportunity—the chance of great
happiness as well as the certainty of death.

This is not easy. Our moods affect our perceptions, as do the
moods of others around us, and there will always be questions
about the reliability of the evidence. Generally it helps to recruit
the observations of others, since our individual perceptions could
be erroneous, and whether the issue has to do with the approach
of a marauding leopard or the possibility of a financial downturn,
the more information we can gather the better off we are. This is
the project of science: to pool the rigorous observations of many
people into a tentative accounting of the world, which will of
course always be subject to revisions arising from fresh observations.

But the group—whether it's a prehistoric band of forty people,
the president's National Security Council, or the American Psychological Association—is not entirely trustworthy either. No
matter how intelligent and well informed its members are, the
group may fall into the grip of collective delusions, frenzies, intellectual fads, or what has been identified in recent decades as
"group think." There seems to be an evolutionary paradox at work
here: human survival in the face of multiple threats depended on
our ability to live in groups, but the imperative of maintaining
group cohesion can sometimes override realism and common

sense, making us hesitate to challenge the consensus or be the bearer of bad news. So, after checking with others, it remains the responsibility of each individual to sift through the received wisdom, insofar as possible, and decide what's worth holding on to. This can require the courage of a Galileo, the iconoclasm of a Darwin or Freud, the diligence of a homicide detective.

At issue is not only knowledge of the world but our survival as individuals and as a species. All the basic technologies ever invented by humans to feed and protect themselves depend on a relentless commitment to hard-nosed empiricism: you cannot assume that your arrowheads will pierce the hide of a bison or that your raft will float just because the omens are propitious and you have been given supernatural reassurance that they will. You have to be sure. Prehistoric humans had to make a careful study of the natural world and the materials it offered them—for example, rocks, clay, plant fibers, animal sinews. Then they had to experiment until, through trial and error, they found what actually works. Without a doubt, throughout our several hundred thousand years of existence on earth, humans have also been guided by superstition, mystical visions, and collective delusions of all sorts. But we got where we are, fanning out over the huge continent of Africa and from there all over the earth, through the strength of the knots we could tie, the sturdiness of shelters and boats, the sharpness of spearheads.

Human intellectual progress, such as it has been, results from our long struggle to see things "as they are," or in the most universally comprehensible way, and not as projections of our own emotions. Thunder is not a tantrum in the sky, disease is not a divine punishment, and not every death or accident results from witchcraft. What we call the Enlightenment and hold on to only tenuously, by our fingernails, is the slow-dawning understanding that the world is unfolding according to its own inner algorithms of cause and effect, probability and chance, without any regard for human feelings.

I realize that after decades of positive thinking the notion of realism, of things as they are, may seem a little quaint. But even in America, the heartland of positive thinking, some stubborn strain of realism has persisted throughout these years of delusion. When the stakes are high enough and the risks obvious, we still turn to people who can be counted on to understand those risks and prepare for worst-case scenarios. A chief of state does not want to hear a general in the field say that he "hopes" to win tomorrow's battle or that he's "visualizing victory"; he or she wants one whose plans include the possibility that things may go very badly, and fall-back positions in case they do. Even that ultra-optimistic president Ronald Reagan invoked realism when dealing with the Soviets, constantly repeating the slogan "Trust, but verify." Magazine editors expect their fact-checkers to assume that a writer's memory is unreliable. We want our airplane pilots to anticipate failed engines as well as happy landings.

In our daily lives, too, all of us, no matter how determinedly upbeat, rely on what psychologist Julie Norem calls "defensive pessimism" to get through the day.[2] Not only pilots need to envision the worst; so does the driver of a car. Should you assume, positively, that no one is going to cut in front of you or, more negatively, be prepared to brake? Most of us would choose a physician who is willing to investigate the most dire possibilities rather than one who is known to settle quickly on an optimistic diagnosis. In matters of the heart as well, a certain level of negativity and suspicion is universally recommended. You may try to project a thoroughly "positive" outlook in order to attract a potential boyfriend, but you are also advised to Google him. When people write to advice columnists about their suspicions as to a spouse's infidelity, they are told not to ignore the warnings and think positively but to confront the problem openly.

One of the most essential and mundane of human activities—taking care of children—requires high levels of anxious vigilance. It would be unwise, even negligent, to assume that teenagers can be counted on to drive carefully and abstain from unsafe sex. To conscientious caretakers, the world is a potential minefield of disasters-in-waiting—tiny plastic toy parts that a baby might swallow, contaminated or unhealthful foods, speeding drivers, pederasts, vicious dogs. Parents might want to be "positive" by advertising a trip to the pediatrician as an opportunity to play with the cool toys in the waiting room rather than an occasion for a painful shot, but they dare not risk assuming that the sudden quiet from the toddlers' room means they are studying with Baby Einstein. Visualize fratricidal stranglings and electric outlets stabbed with forks: this is how we have reproduced our genomes.

When our children are old enough, and if we can afford to, we send them to college, where despite the recent proliferation of courses on "happiness" and "positive psychology," the point is to acquire the skills not of positive thinking but of *critical* thinking, and critical thinking is inherently skeptical. The best students—and in good colleges, also the most successful—are the ones who raise sharp questions, even at the risk of making a professor momentarily uncomfortable. Whether the subject is literature or engineering, graduates should be capable of challenging authority figures, going against the views of their classmates, and defending novel points of view. This is not because academics value contrarianism for its own sake but because they recognize that a society needs people who will do exactly what the gurus of positive thinking warn us to avoid—"overintellectualize" and ask hard questions. Physicians are among the highly educated professionals who dare not risk the comforts of positive thinking in their daily work, and as one of them, author and surgeon Atul Gawande, has written: "Whether one is fighting a cancer, an insurgency or just an unyielding problem at work, the prevailing wisdom is that thinking positive is the key—The Secret, even—to success. But the key, it seems to me, is actually negative thinking: looking for, and sometimes expecting, failure."[3]

Realism—to the point of defensive pessimism—is a prerequisite not only for human survival but for all animal species. Watch almost any wild creature for a few moments and you will be impressed, above all, by its vigilance. The cormorant restlessly scans the water for unexpected splashes; the deer cocks its head to pick up stray sounds and raises a foot in preparation for flight. Many animals—from monkeys to birds—augment their individual watchfulness by living in groups so that many eyes can be on the lookout for intruders, many voices raised in an alarm call, should one approach. In its insistence that we concentrate on happy outcomes rather than on lurking hazards, positive thinking contradicts one of our most fundamental instincts, one that we share not only with other primates and mammals but with reptiles, insects, and fish.

The rationale of the positive thinkers has been that the world is not, or at least no longer is, the dangerous place we imagined it to be. This is how Mary Baker Eddy saw it: the universe was "Supply" and "Abundance" made available to everyone by a benevolent deity. Sin, crime, disease, poverty—all these were "errors" wrought by minds that had fallen out of resonance with the cosmic vibrations of generosity and love. A hundred years later, Martin Seligman, the founder of positive psychology, was describing anxiety and pessimism as unhelpful vestiges of our Paleolithic past, when our ancestors scrambled to avoid predators, "flood, and famine." Today, however, "goods and services are plentiful," as he put it;

there is enough to go around, and we can finally let our guard down. Any lingering dissatisfaction is, as Eddy would have said, a kind of error—correctible through the right self-help techniques and optimism exercises.

But has the human outlook really been improving over time? For affluent individuals in peaceful settings, decidedly yes, but our overall situation is as perilous as it has ever been. Even some of the most positive-thinking evangelical pastors have recently acknowledged the threat of global warming. The notion that the world's supply of oil may have peaked is no longer the province of a few environmentally minded kooks; "doomsters" are gaining respectability. Everywhere we look, the forests are falling, the deserts are advancing, the supply of animal species is declining. The seas are rising, and there are fewer and fewer fish in them to eat.

Over the last couple of decades, as icebergs sank and levels of debt mounted, dissidents from the prevailing positive-thinking consensus were isolated, mocked, or urged to overcome their perverse attachment to negative thoughts. Within the United States, any talk of intractable problems like poverty could be dismissed as a denial of America's greatness. Any complaints of economic violence could be derided as the "whining" of self-selected victims.

It's easy to see positive thinking as a uniquely American form of naïveté, but it is neither uniquely American nor endearingly naïve. In vastly different settings, positive thinking has been a tool of political repression worldwide. We tend to think that tyrants rule through fear—fear of the secret police, of torture, detention, the gulag—but some of the world's most mercilessly authoritarian regimes have also demanded constant optimism and cheer from their subjects. In his book *Shah of Shahs,* about life under the shah of Iran, who ruled until the revolution of 1979, Ryszard Kapuscinski tells the story of a translator who managed to get a poem published despite the fact that it included the seditious line "Now is the time of sorrow, of darkest night." The translator was "elated" at being able to get the poem past the censors, "in this country where everything is supposed to inspire optimism, blossoming, smiles—suddenly 'the time of sorrow'! Can you imagine?"[4]

Soviet-style Communism, which we do not usually think of as a cheerful sort of arrangement, exemplified the use of positive thinking as a means of social control. Writing of the former Yugoslavia at the beginning of the twenty-first century, Dubravka Ugresic observed that "former communists, modern capitalists, nationalists, religious fanatics" were all picking up on the fresh breeze of positivity from the West. "They have all become optimists." But this was hardly something new, she went on, because "optimism has a stain on its ideological record. . . . If anything has survived Stalinism itself, it is the Stalinist demand for optimism."[5] In the Soviet Union, as in the Eastern European states and North Korea, the censors required upbeat art, books, and films, meaning upbeat heroes, plots about fulfilling production quotas, and endings promising a glorious revolutionary future. Czechoslovakian literature was suffused with "blind optimism"; North Korean short stories still beam with "relentless optimism." In the Soviet Union itself, "being charged with a lack of historical optimism meant being charged with distortion of the truth or transmission of false truths. Pessimism and ideological wavering meant the same thing. . . . In various disputes, the possibility of an alienated and lonely hero in socialism was forbidden in the name of the demands for historical optimism and a positive hero."[6]

The penalties for negative thinking were real. Not to be positive and optimistic was to be "defeatist," and, as Ugresic writes of the Soviet Union, "*defeatists* paid for the sin of defeatism. Accusing someone of *spreading defeatism* condemned him to several years in Stalinist camps."[7] In his 1968 novel, *The Joke*, the Czech writer Milan Kundera has a character send a postcard bearing the line "Optimism is the opium of the people," for which the character is accused of being an enemy of the people and sentenced to hard labor in the coal mines. Kundera himself was punished for daring to write *The Joke*. He was expelled from the Communist Party, saw his works removed from libraries and bookstores, and was banned from traveling to the West.

American preachers of positive thinking would no doubt be appalled to find themselves mentioned in the same breath or even the same book as Stalinist censors and propagandists. After all, Americans exalt individual success, which was not a Communist ideal, and no one gets hauled off to labor camps for ignoring their teachings. But even among American proponents of positive thinking, you can find a faint uneasiness about its role as a mental discipline, a form of self-hypnosis involving affirmations, visualizations, and tightly focused thoughts. "Don't think of 'thought control' as a repressive tool out of George Orwell's 1984," John Templeton advised the readers of one of his self-help books. "Rather, think of it as a positive force that will leave your mind clearer, more directed, and more effective."[8]

The big advantage of the American approach to positive thinking has been that people can be counted on to impose it on themselves. Stalinist regimes used the state apparatus—schools, secret police, and so on—to enforce optimism; capitalist democracies leave this job to the market. In the West, as we have seen, the leading proponents of positive thinking are entrepreneurs in their own right, marketing their speeches, books, and DVDs to anyone willing to buy them. Large companies may make their employees listen to the speeches and may advise them to read the books; they may fire people who persist in a "negative attitude." But it's ultimately up to the individual to embrace positive thinking and do the hard work of attitude adjustment and maintenance on him- or herself. And judging from the sales of motivational products and the popularity of figures like Oprah and Osteen, this is a task that large numbers of Americans have eagerly undertaken on their own.

Yet, as the cover story of the January 2009 issue of *Psychology Today* acknowledges, the American infatuation with positive thinking has not made us happier. Lumping academic positive psychology and the ever-growing host of "self-appointed experts" together into what he calls the "happiness movement," the writer notes that, "according to some measures, as a nation we've grown sadder and more anxious during the same years that the happiness movement has flourished; perhaps that's why we've eagerly bought up its offerings."[9] This finding should hardly come as a surprise: positive thinking did not abolish the need for constant vigilance; it only turned that vigilance inward. Instead of worrying that one's roof might collapse or one's job be terminated, positive thinking encourages us to worry about the negative expectations themselves and subject them to continual revision. It ends up imposing a mental discipline as exacting as that of the Calvinism it replaced—the endless work of self-examination and self-control or, in the case of positive thinking, self-hypnosis. It requires, as historian Donald Meyer puts it, "constant repetition of its spirit lifters, constant alertness against impossibility perspectives, constant monitoring of rebellions of body and mind against control."[10]

This is a burden that we can finally, in good conscience, put down. The effort of positive "thought control," which is always presented as such a life preserver, has become a potentially deadly weight—obscuring judgment and shielding us from vital information. Sometimes we need to heed our fears and negative thoughts, and at all times we need to be alert to the world outside ourselves, even when that includes absorbing bad news and entertaining the views of "negative" people. As we should have learned by now, it is dangerous not to.

A vigilant realism does not foreclose the pursuit of happiness; in fact, it makes it possible. How can we expect to improve our situation without addressing the actual circumstances we find ourselves in? Positive thinking seeks to convince us that such external factors are incidental compared with one's internal state or attitude or mood. We have seen how the coaches and gurus dismiss real-world problems as "excuses" for failure and how positive psychologists have tended to minimize the "C," for circumstances, in their happiness equation. It's true that subjective factors like determination are critical to survival and that individuals sometimes triumph over nightmarish levels of adversity. But mind does not automatically prevail over matter, and to ignore the role of difficult circumstances—or worse, attribute them to our own thoughts— is to slide toward the kind of depraved smugness Rhonda Byrne expressed when confronted with the tsunami of 2004. Citing the law of attraction, she stated that disasters like tsunamis can happen only to people who are "on the same frequency as the event."[11]

Worldwide, the most routine obstacle to human happiness is poverty. To the extent that happiness surveys can be believed, they consistently show that the world's happiest countries tend also to be among the richest. While the United States ranks 23rd and the United Kingdom 41st, for example, India comes in a gloomy 125th out of 178 nations.[12] Some recent studies find furthermore that, within countries, richer people tend to be happier, with about 90 percent of Americans in households earning at least $250,000 a year reporting being "very happy," compared with only 42 percent of people in households earning less than $30,000.[13] When the New York Times surveyed New York neighborhoods in 2009, it found that the happiest areas were also the most affluent and, not coincidentally, the most thickly supplied

with cafés, civic associations, theaters, and opportunities for social interaction. The least happy neighborhood was a part of the
Bronx characterized by abandoned buildings, mounds of uncol-
lected garbage, and the highest unemployment rate in the city.[14]

For centuries, or at least since the Protestant Reformation,
Western economic elites have flattered themselves with the idea
that poverty is a voluntary condition. The Calvinist saw it as a result of sloth and other bad habits; the positive thinker blamed it
on a willful failure to embrace abundance. This victim-blaming
approach meshed neatly with the prevailing economic conserva-
tism of the last two decades. Welfare recipients were pushed out
into low-wage jobs, supposedly, in part, to boost their self-esteem;
laid-off and soon-to-be-laid-off workers were subjected to motivational speakers and exercises. But the economic meltdown should
have undone, once and for all, the idea of poverty as a personal
shortcoming or dysfunctional state of mind. The lines at unemployment offices and churches offering free food include strivers
as well as slackers, habitual optimists as well as the chronically
depressed. When and if the economy recovers we can never allow
ourselves to forget how widespread our vulnerability is, how easy
it is to spiral down toward destitution.

Happiness is not, of course, guaranteed even to those who are
affluent, successful, and well loved. But that happiness is not the
inevitable outcome of happy circumstances does not mean we can
find it by journeying inward to revise our thoughts and feelings.
The threats we face are real and can be vanquished only by shaking off self-absorption and taking action in the world. Build up
the levees, get food to the hungry, find the cure, strengthen the
"first responders"! We will not succeed at all these things, certainly
not all at once, but—if I may end with my own personal secret of
happiness—we can have a good time trying.

Notes

_____

Introduction

1. "Happiness Is 'Infectious' in Network of Friends: Collective—Not Just Individual—Phenomenon," *ScienceDaily*, Dec. 5, 2008, http://www.science daily.com/releases/2008/12/081205094506.htm.

2. Daniel Kahneman and Alan B. Krueger, "Developments in the Measurement of Subjective Well-Being," *Journal of Economic Perspectives* 20 (2006): 3–24.

3. "Psychologist Produces the First-Ever 'World Map of Happiness,'" *ScienceDaily*, Nov. 14, 2006, http://www.sciencedaily.com/releases/2006/11/061113093726.htm.

4. http://rankingamerica.wordpress.com/2009/01/11/the-us-ranks-150th-in -planet-happiness/, Jan. 11, 2009.

5. Godfrey Hodgson, *The Myth of American Exceptionalism* (New Haven: Yale University Press, 2009), 113; Paul Krugman, "America the Boastful," *Foreign Affairs*, May–June 1998.

6. 2000 State of the Union Address, Jan. 27, 2000, http://www.washingtonpost .com/wp-srv/politics/special/states/docs/sou00.htm; Geoff Elliott, "Dubya's 60th Takes the Cake," *Weekend Australian*, July 8, 2006; Woodward, quoting

Rice, *Meet the Press* transcript, Dec. 21, 2008, http://today.msnbc.msn.com/id/28337897/.

7. Quoted in Karen A. Cerulo, *Never Saw It Coming: Cultural Challenges to Envisioning the Worst* (Chicago: University of Chicago Press, 2006), 18.

8. Cerulo, *Never Saw It Coming*, 239.

9. Hope Yen, "Death in Streets Took a Back Seat to Dinner," *Seattle Times*, Oct. 25, 2005.

ONE. Smile or Die: The Bright Side of Cancer

1. Susan M. Love, with Karen Lindsey, *Dr. Susan Love's Breast Book* (Cambridge: Perseus, 2000), 380–81.

2. Gina Kolata, "In Long Drive to Cure Cancer, Advances Have Been Elusive," *New York Times*, April 24, 2009.

3. Stephen C. Fehr, "Cheerfully Fighting a Killer; Upbeat Race for Cure Nets $3 Million for Cancer Research," *Washington Post*, June 4, 2000.

4. Charla Hudson Honea, *The First Year of the Rest of Your Life: Reflections for Survivors of Breast Cancer* (Cleveland: Pilgrim Press, 1997), 6.

5. Jane E. Brody, "Thriving after Life's Bum Rap," *New York Times*, Aug. 14, 2007.

6. Ann McNerney, *The Gift of Cancer: A Call to Awakening* (Baltimore: Resonant Publishing, n.d.), 183, vii.

7. Honea, *The First Year*, 25, 36, 81.

8. http://www.cfah.org/hbns/newsrelease/women3-07-01.cfm.

9. http://www.nugget.ca/webapp/sitepages/content.asp?contentid=537743&catname=Local+News.

10. http://ezinearticles.com/?Breast-Cancer-Prevention-Tips&id=199110.

11. O. Carl Simonton, Stephanie Matthews-Simonton, and James L. Creighton, *Getting Well Again* (New York: Bantam, 1992), 43.

12. Bernie S. Siegel, *Love, Medicine, and Miracles: Lessons Learned about Self-Healing from a Surgeon's Experience with Exceptional Patients* (New York: Harper and Row, 1986), 77.

13. Simonton et al., *Getting Well Again*, 144–45.

14. J. C. Coyne, M. Stefanek, and S. C. Palmer, "Psychotherapy and Survival in Cancer: The Conflict between Hope and Evidence," *Psychological Bulletin* 133 (2007): 367–94.

15. http://www.bio-medicine.org/medicine-news-1/Cancer-survival-is-not-influenced-by-a-patients-emotional-status-4214-2/.

16. John L. Marshall, "Time to Shift the Focus of the War: It Is Not All about the Enemy," *Journal of Clinical Oncology* 27(2009): 168–69.

17. E. Y. Lin et al., "Macrophages Regulate the Angiogenic Switch in a Mouse Model of Breast Cancer," *Cancer Research* 66 (2006): 11238–46.

18. Gary Stix, "A Malignant Flame," *Scientific American*, July 2007, 46–49.

19. "Instead of Fighting Breast Cancer, Immune Cell Promotes Its Spread," *Science Daily*, April 26, 2009, http://www.sciencedaily.com/releases/2009/04/090422103554.htm.

20. Howard Tennet and Glenn Affleck, "Benefit Finding and Benefit Reminding," *Handbook of Positive Psychology*, ed. C. R. Snyder and Shane J. Lopez (New York: Oxford University Press, 2002).

21. Quoted in Karen A. Cerulo, *Never Saw It Coming: Cultural Challenges to Envisioning the Worst* (Chicago: University of Chicago Press, 2006), 118.

22. Tennet and Affleck, op. cit.

23. M. Dittman, "Benefit-Finding Doesn't Always Mean Improved Lives for Breast Cancer Patients," *APAOnline*, Feb. 2004.

24. Deepak Chopra, "Positive Attitude Helps Overcome Cancer Recurrence," http://health.yahoo.com/experts/deepak/92/positive-attitude-helps-overcome-cancer-recurrence, April 17, 2007.

25. "A Positive Attitude Does Not Help Cancer Outcome," http://www.medicalnewstoday.com/medicalnews.php?newsid=5780, Feb. 9, 2004.

26. Cynthia Rittenberg, "Positive Thinking: An Unfair Burden for Cancer Patients," *Supportive Care in Cancer* 3 (1995): 37–39.

27. Jimmie Holland, "The Tyranny of Positive Thinking," http://www.leukemia-lymphoma.org/all_page?item_id=7038&viewmode=print.

TWO. The Years of Magical Thinking

1. Joseph Anzack, *CNN American Morning*, May 16, 2007.

2. Barry Corbet, "Embedded: A No-Holds-Barred Report from Inside a Nursing Home," *AARP: The Magazine*, Jan.–Feb. 2007, http://www.aarpmagazine.org/health/embedded.html.

3. Scott McLemee, "Motivation and Its Discontents," www.insidehighered.com, Feb. 28, 2007.

4. Dale Carnegie, *How to Win Friends and Influence People* (New York: Pocket Books, 1982), 70, 61, 64.

5. Arlie Russell Hochschild, *The Managed Heart: Commercialization of Human Feeling* (Berkeley: University of California Press, 1983).

6. William H. Whyte, *The Organization Man* (Philadelphia: University of Pennsylvania Press, 2002), 46–47, 14.

7. Tom Rath and Donald O. Clifton, *How Full Is Your Bucket? Positive Strategies for Work and Life* (New York: Gallup Press, 2004), 47.

8. Quoted on the American Management Association's Web site, http://www.amanet.org/books/book.cfm?isbn=9780814405826.

9. T. Harv Eker, *Secrets of the Millionaire Mind: Mastering the Inner Game of Wealth* (New York: HarperBusiness, 2005), 101.

10. Jeffrey Gitomer, *Little Gold Book of YES!* (Upper Saddle River: FT Press, 2007), 138.

11. http://guruknowledge.org/articles/255/1/The-Power-of-Negative-Thinking/The-Power-of-Negative-Thinking.html.

12. Gitomer, *Little Gold Book*, 45.

13. Judy Braley, "Creating a Positive Attitude," http://ezinearticles.com/?Creating-a-Positive-Attitude&id=759618.

14. Quoted in http://www.nationmaster.com/encyclopedia/The-Secret-(2006-film).

15. Rhonda Byrne, *The Secret* (New York: Atria Books/Beyond Words, 2006), 116.

16. Jerry Adler, "Decoding 'The Secret,'" *Newsweek*, March 5, 2007.

17. Eker, *Secrets*, 67; Vitale quoted in Byrne, *The Secret*, 48.

18. Catherine L. Albanese, *A Republic of Mind and Spirit: A Cultural History of American Metaphysical Religion* (New Haven: Yale University Press, 2007), 7.

19. *Larry King Live*, CNN, Nov. 2, 2006.

20. http://www.globalpsychics.com/empowering-you/practical-magic/prosperity.shtml.

21. Michael J. Losier, *Law of Attraction: The Science of Attracting More of What You Want and Less of What You Don't* (Victoria: Michael J. Losier Enterprises, 2006), 13.

22. Napoleon Hill, *Think and Grow Rich!* (San Diego: Aventine Press, 2004), 21.

23. Michael Shermer, "The (Other) Secret," *Scientific American*, July 2007, 39.

24. Byrne, *The Secret*, 21.

25. http://ezinearticles.com/?The-Law-of-Attraction-and-Quantum-Physics&id=223148.

26. Michael Shermer, "Quantum Quackery," *Scientific American*, Dec. 20, 2004.

27. Byrne, *The Secret*, 88.

THREE. The Dark Roots of American Optimism

1. Ann Douglas, *The Feminization of American Culture* (New York: Avon, 1977), 145.
2. Thomas Hooker, quoted in Perry Miller, ed., *The American Puritans: Their Prose and Poetry* (New York: Columbia University Press, 1982), 154.
3. Miller, *American Puritans*, 241.
4. Quoted in Noel L. Brann, "The Problem of Distinguishing Religious Guilt from Religious Melancholy in the English Renaissance," *Journal of the Rocky Mountain Medieval and Renaissance Association* (1980): 70.
5. Julius H. Rubin, *Religious Melancholy and Protestant Experience in America* (New York: Oxford University Press, 1994), 161.
6. Max Weber, *The Protestant Ethic and the Spirit of Capitalism* (New York: Dover, 2003), 168.
7. William Bradford, quoted in Stephen Fender and Arnold Goldman, eds., *American Literature in Context* (New York: Routledge, 1983), 45.
8. Personal communication, Jan. 10, 2009.
9. Quoted in Catherine L. Albanese, *A Republic of Mind and Spirit: A Cultural History of American Metaphysical Religion* (New Haven: Yale University Press, 2007), 165.
10. Quoted in Albanese, *Republic of Mind and Spirit*, 167.
11. Quoted in Gillian Gill, *Mary Baker Eddy* (Cambridge: Perseus, 1998), 43.
12. Quoted in Caroline Fraser, *God's Perfect Child: Living and Dying in the Christian Science Church* (New York: Metropolitan, 1999), 34.
13. Quoted in Barbara Ehrenreich and Deirdre English, *For Her Own Good: 150 Years of the Experts' Advice to Women* (New York: Anchor, 1989), 103.
14. Douglas, *Feminization*, 170.
15. Quoted in Anne Harrington, *The Cure Within: A History of Mind-Body Medicine* (New York: Norton, 2008), 112.
16. Douglas, *Feminization*, 170.
17. Barbara Sicherman, "The Paradox of Prudence: Mental Health in the Gilded Age," *Journal of American History* 62 (1976): 880–912.
18. Quoted in Douglas, *Feminization*, 104.
19. Gill, *Mary Baker Eddy*, 33.
20. Quoted in Robert D. Richardson, *William James: In the Maelstrom of American Modernism* (Boston: Houghton Mifflin, 2006), 86.

21. Roy M. Anker, *Self-Help and Popular Religion in Early American Culture: An Interpretive Guide* (Westport: Greenwood Press, 1999), 190.

22. Gill, *Mary Baker Eddy*, 128.

23. Richardson, *William James*, 275.

24. William James, *The Varieties of Religious Experience: A Study in Human Nature* (New York: Modern Library, 2002), 109.

25. Ibid., 104.

26. Ibid., 109.

27. Ibid., 109, 111n.

28. Quoted in Fraser, *God's Perfect Child*, 195.

29. Micki McGee, *Self-Help, Inc.: Makeover Culture in American Life* (New York: Oxford University Press, 2005), 142.

30. http://www.bripblap.com/2007/stopping-negative-thoughts/.

31. Napoleon Hill, *Think and Grow Rich!* (San Diego: Aventine Press, 2004), 52, 29, 71, 28, 30, 74.

32. Norman Vincent Peale, back cover quote on Fenwicke Holmes, *Ernest Holmes: His Life and Times* (New York Dodd, Mead, 1970), http://self-improvement-ebooks.com/books/ehhlat.php.

33. Norman Vincent Peale, *The Positive Principle Today* (New York: Random House, 1994), 289.

34. Donald Meyer, *The Positive Thinkers: Popular Religious Psychology from Mary Baker Eddy to Norman Vincent Peale and Ronald Reagan* (Middletown: Wesleyan University Press, 1998), 268.

35. Norman Vincent Peale, *The Power of Positive Thinking* (New York: Random House, 1994), 28.

36. T. Harv Eker, *Secrets of the Millionaire Mind* (New York: Harper Business, 2005), 94.

37. Quoted in McGee, *Self-Help, Inc.*, 143.

38. Ibid., 142.

39. Jeffrey Gitomer, *Little Gold Book*, 164.

40. Ibid., 165.

41. Ibid., 169.

42. Quoted in Meyer, *Positive Thinkers*, 80.

FOUR. Motivating Business and the Business of Motivation

1. Steven Winn, "Overcome that Gnawing Fear of Success! Seize Your Share of the American Dream! You—Yes, You, Ma'am—Can Do It, at a One-Day Gath-

ering That's Equal Parts Boot Camp, Tent Revival, Pep Rally and Group Therapy," *San Francisco Chronicle*, May 24, 2004.

2. Rick Romell, "Selling Motivation Amounts to Big Business: Self-Help Guru Finds Success Again with His New Firm," *Milwaukee Journal Sentinel* online, May 21, 2007.

3. Jonathan Black, *Yes You Can! Behind the Hype and Hustle of the Motivation Biz* (NY: Bloomsbury Publishing, 2006).

4. William Lee Miller, "Some Negative Thinking about Norman Vincent Peale," originally published in *Reporter*, Jan. 13, 1955, http://george.loper.org/trends/2005/Aug/955.html.

5. Rob Spiegel, "The Hidden Rule of Positive Thinking," www.businessknowhow.com/startup/hidden.htm.

6. Carol V. R. George, *God's Salesman: Norman Vincent Peale and the Power of Positive Thinking* (New York: Oxford University Press, 1994), 233.

7. George, *God's Salesman*, 124.

8. Stephanie Saul, "Gimme an Rx! Cheerleaders Pep Up Drug Sales," *New York Times*, Nov. 28, 2005.

9. Jerry Pounds, "The Great Motivational Myth," http://www.management-issues.com/2006/5/25/opinion/the-great-motivational-myth.asp.

10. Karl Vick, "Team-Building or Torture? Court Will Decide," *Washington Post*, April 13, 2008.

11. Robin Leidner, *Fast Food, Fast Talk: Service Work and the Routinization of Everyday Life* (Berkeley: University of California Press, 1993), 65, 100–101, 104.

12. Stephen Butterfield, *Amway: The Cult of Free Enterprise* (Boston: South End Press, 1985), 100.

13. Ibid., 28–29, 36–37.

14. Jonathan Black, *Yes You Can!*, 180.

15. Quoted in Rakesh Khurana, *From Higher Aims to Hired Hands: The Social Transformation of American Business Schools and the Unfulfilled Promise of Management as a Profession* (Princeton: Princeton University Press, 2007), 303.

16. Khurana, *From Higher Aims*, 320–21, 325.

17. Clive Thompson, "Apocalypse Now: As the Year 2000 Approaches, Politicians and Business Leaders Are Getting Ready for the End of the World. Things Have Never Looked Better," *Canadian Business and Current Affairs*, Jan. 1996, 29–33.

18. Jennifer Reingold and Ryan Underwood, "Was *Built to Last* Built to Last?" *Fast Company*, Nov. 2004, 103.

19. Michelle Conlin, "Religion in the Workplace," *BusinessWeek*, Nov. 1, 1999, 150.

20. Craig Lambert, "The Cult of the Charismatic CEO," *Harvard Magazine*, Sept.– Oct. 2002.

21. Dennis Toruish and Ashly Pinnington, "Transformational Leadership, Corporate Cultism, and the Spirituality Paradigm: An Unholy Trinity in the Workplace?" *Human Relations* 55 (2002): 147.

22. Conlon, "Religion in the Workplace."

23. Gay Hendricks and Kate Ludeman, *The Corporate Mystic: A Guidebook for Visionaries with Their Feet on the Ground* (New York: Bantam, 1996), xvii.

24. Frank Rose and Wilton Woods, "A New Age for Business?" *Fortune*, Oct. 8, 1990, 157.

25. Thompson, "Apocalypse Now."

26. Mark Gimein, "Now That We Live in a Tom Peters World . . . Has Tom Peters Gone Crazy?" *Fortune*, Nov. 13, 2000.

27. Jack Welch, with John A. Byrne, *Jack: Straight from the Gut* (New York: Business Plus, 2003), 436.

28. Jeffrey E. Lewin and Wesley J. Johnston, "Competitiveness," *Competitiveness Review*, Jan. 1, 2000.

29. Louis Uchitelle, *The Disposable American: Layoffs and Their Consequences* (New York: Knopf, 2006), x.

30. Henry S. Farber, "What Do We Know about Job Loss in the United States? Evidence from the Displaced Workers' Survey, 1984–2005," Working Paper 498, Princeton University Industrial Relations Section, Jan. 5, 2005.

31. Quoted in Carrie M. Lane, "A Company of One: White-Collar Unemployment in a Global Economy," unpublished ms., 131.

32. Quoted in Gaenor Vaida, "The Guru's Guru," *Sunday Times* (South Africa), July 6, 2003.

33. Lloyd Grove, "The Power of Positive Buying; Feeling Unmotivated? This Mug's for You," *Washington Post*, Dec. 31, 1994.

34. http://64.233.169.104/search?q=cache:_icxqiKivO0J; www.workplacecoaching .com/pdf/HistoryofCoaching.pdf+%22history+of+coaching%22&hl=en&ct =clnk&cd=1&gl=us2.

35. Richard Reeves, "Let's Get Motivated," *Time*, May 2, 1994.

36. Lloyd Grove, "Power Of Positive Buying."

37. William A. Davis, "Stores Cash in on Selling Success," *Boston Globe,* Aug. 1, 1994.

38. Rayna Katz, "Planners Face a Different-Looking Future, Reports Say," *Meeting News,* Sept. 18, 2000, http://www.allbusiness.com/transportation -communications-electric-gas/4227180-1.html.

39. http://www.cprcoaching.com/employee_retention_team_building.html.

40. Spencer Johnson, *Who Moved My Cheese?* (New York: Putnam, 1998), 35, 71.

41. Ibid., 57.

42. Jill Andresky Fraser, *White-Collar Sweatshop: The Deterioration of Work and Its Rewards in Corporate America* (New York: Norton, 2001), 195.

43. John Balzar, "Losing a Job: From Great Depression to Reinvention, *Los Angeles Times,* Oct. 20, 1993.

44. Lane, "Company of One."

45. Fraser, *White-Collar Sweatshop,* 191, 193.

46. Jennifer M. Howard, "Can Teams Survive Downsizing?", http://www .qualitydigest.com/may/downsize.html.

47. Paul Solman, "The Right Choice?," *PBS Online NewsHour,* March 22, 1996, http://www.pbs.org/newshour/bb/economy/att_layoffs_3-22.html.

48. http://www.thesykesgrp.com/Teamtrg01.htm.

49. Fraser, *White-Collar Sweatshop,* 191–92.

FIVE. God Wants You to Be Rich

1. Abe Levy, "Megachurches Growing in Number and Size," AP, via SFGate .com, Feb. 3, 2006, http://www.religionnewsblog.com/13512/megachurches -growing-in-number-and-size.

2. David Van Biema and Jeff Chu, "Does God Want You to Be Rich?" *Time,* Sept. 18, 2006, 48.

3. Gabriel N. Lischak, "The Rise of the 'Megachurch': A New Phenomenon Is Taking Shape in America—One That Is Radically Redefining the 'Christian Experience,'" Jan. 6, 2006, http://www.realtruth.org/articles/418-trotm-print .html.

4. http://www.thechurchreport.com/mag_article.php?mid=875&mname =January.

5. William Lee Miller, "Some Negative Thinking about Norman Vincent Peale," originally published in *Reporter,* Jan. 13, 1955, http://george.loper.org/trends/ 2005/Aug/955.html.

6. Joel Osteen, *Your Best Life Now: 7 Steps to Living at Your Full Potential* (New York: Faith Words, 2004), 183.

7. Ted Olsen, "Weblog: Kenneth Hagin, 'Word of Faith' Preacher, Dies at 86," Sept. 1, 2003, http://www.christianitytoday.com/ct/2003/septemberweb-only/9-22-11.0.html?start=1.

8. Osteen, *Your Best Life Now*, 5, 101, 41.

9. Ibid., 112.

10. Dennis Voskuil, *Mountains into Goldmines: Robert Schuller and the Gospel of Success* (Grand Rapids: Eerdmans, 1983), 80.

11. Chris Lehmann, "Pentecostalism for the Exurbs: Joel Osteen's God Really Wants You to Dress Well, Stand Up Straight, and Get a Convenient Parking Space," Jan. 2, 2008, http://www.slate.com/id/2180590/.

12. Edwene Gaines, *The Four Spiritual Laws of Prosperity: A Simple Guide to Unlimited Abundance* (New York: Rodale, 2005), 88.

13. D. R. McConnell, *A Different Gospel* (Peabody: Hendrickson, 1988).

14. Shayne Lee, "Prosperity Theology: T. D. Jakes and the Gospel of the Almighty Dollar," *Cross Currents*, June 22, 2007, 227.

15. Milmon F. Harrison, "Prosperity Here and Now: Synthesizing New Thought with Charismatic Christianity, the Word of Faith Movement Promises Its Members the Good Life," http://www.beliefnet.com/Faiths/Christianity/2000/05/Prosperity-Here-And-Now.aspx.

16. Ibid.

17. Van Biema and Chu, "Does God Want You to Be Rich?," 48.

18. See John Jackson, *PastorPreneur: Pastors and Entrepreneurs Answer the Call* (Friendswood: Baxter, 2003).

19. Quoted in Scott Thumma, "Exploring the Megachurch Phenomenon: Their Characteristics and Cultural Context," http://hirr.hartsem.edu/bookshelf/thumma_article2.html.

20. Bill Hybels, "Commentary: Building a Church on Marketing Surveys," excerpted from *Christian News*, July 1991, http://www.rapidnet.com/~jbeard/bdm/exposes/hybels/news.htm.

21. Witold Rybczynski, "An Anatomy of Megachurches: The New Look for Places of Worship," Oct. 10, 2005, http://www.slate.com/id/2127615/.

22. Frances Fitzgerald, "Come One, Come All: Building a Megachurch in New England," *New Yorker*, Dec. 3, 2007, 46; Denis Haack, "Bruce Bezaire: Meticulous Renderings of Glory," http://ransomfellowship.org/articledetail.asp?AID=21&B=Denis%20Haack&TID=6.

23. Quoted in Lischak, "Rise of the 'Megachurch.'"
24. Quoted in Van Biema and Chu, "Does God Want You to Be Rich?"
25. "Jesus, CEO," *Economist*, Dec. 20, 2005, http://www.economist.com/world/unitedstates/PrinterFriendly.cfm?story_id=5323597.
26. Felix Salmon, "Market Movers," Jan. 24, 2008, http://www.portfolio.com/views/blogs/market-movers/2008/01/24/davos-surprise-rick-warren; Malcolm Gladwell, "The Cellular Church: How Rick Warren's Congregation Grew," *New Yorker*, Sept. 12, 2005, 60.
27. Gustav Niebuhr, "Megachurches," *New York Times*, April 18, 1995.
28. Osteen, *Your Best Life Now*, 11.
29. Dennis Tourish and Ashly Pinnington, "Transformational Leadership, Corporate Cultism, and the Spirituality Paradigm: An Unholy Trinity in the Workplace?," *Human Relations* 55 (2002): 147.
30. "Jesus, CEO."
31. Quoted in Voskuil, *Mountains into Goldmines*, 78.
32. Osteen, *Your Best Life Now*, 298.

six. Positive Psychology: The Science of Happiness

1. Martin E. P. Seligman, *Authentic Happiness: Using the New Positive Psychology to Realize Your Potential for Lasting Fulfillment* (New York: The Free Press, 2002), 24; Dorothy Wade, "Happy Yet?," *Australian Magazine*, Oct. 22, 2005, 39.
2. Strawberry Saroyan, "Happy Days Are Here Again," *Elle*, Dec. 1998.
3. Quoted in Jennifer Senior, "Some Dark Thoughts on Happiness," *New York*, July 17, 2006.
4. Robert Biswas-Diener and Ben Dean, *Positive Psychology Coaching: Putting the Science of Happiness to Work for Your Clients* (New York: Wiley, 2007), 12, 31.
5. John Templeton Foundation, Capabilities Report, 2002, 82.
6. Patrick B. Kavanaugh, Lyle D. Danuloff, Robert E. Erard, Marvin Hyman, and Janet L. Pallas, "Psychology: A Profession and Practice at Risk," July 1994, www.academyprojects.org/lempa1.htm; Ilana DeBare, "Career Coaches Help You Climb to the Top: 'Personal Trainers' for Workers New Fiscal Fitness Craze," *San Francisco Chronicle*, May 4, 1998.
7. Seligman, *Authentic Happiness*, ix.
8. Joshua Freedman, "An Interview with Martin E. P. Seligman, Ph.D.," *EQ Today*, Fall 2000 http://www.eqtoday.com/optimism/seligman.html.

9. Wade, "Happy Yet?," 39.

10. Ed Diener and Martin E. P. Seligman, "Beyond Money: Toward an Economy of Wellbeing," *Psychological Science in the Public Interest* 5, no. 1 (2004).

11. John Lanchester, "Pursuing Happiness: Two Scholars Explore the Fragility of Contentment," *New Yorker,* Feb. 27, 2006.

12. Seligman, *Authentic Happiness,* 39.

13. Ibid., 28, 38, 43, 103.

14. Ibid., 119, 120–21.

15. Ibid., 129, 133.

16. Ibid., 45.

17. Ibid., 129.

18. Barbara Held, "The Negative Side of Positive Psychology," *Journal of Humanistic Psychology* 44 (Winter 2004): 9–46.

19. Biswas-Diener and Dean, *Positive Psychology Coaching,* 31.

20. Sonja Lyubomirsky, Laura King, and Ed Diener, "The Benefits of Frequent Positive Affect: Does Happiness Lead to Success?," *Psychological Bulletin* 131 (2005): 803–55.

21. Mike McGrath, "When Back Pain Starts in Your Head: Is Repressed Anger Causing Your Back Pain?" http://www.prevention.com/cda/article/when-back -pain-starts-in-your-head/727b7e643f803110VgnVCM10000013281eac____/ health/conditions.treatments/back.pain.

22. Seligman, *Authentic Happiness,* 3. Deborah D. Danner, David A. Snowdon, and Wallace V. Friesen, "Findings from the Nun Study, University of Kentucky," *Journal of Personality and Social Psychology* 80 (2001): 804–13.

23. Gina Kolata, "Research Links Writing Style to the Risk of Alzheimer's," *New York Times,* Feb. 21, 1996, http://www.nytimes.com/1996/02/21/us/research -links-writing-style-to-the-risk-of-alzheimers.html?sec=health.

24. LeeAnne Harker and Dacher Keltner, "Expressions of Positive Emotion in Women's College Yearbook Pictures and Their Relationship to Personality and Life Outcomes across Adulthood," University of California, Berkeley, http://ist-socrates.berkeley.edu/~keltner/publications/harker.jpsp.2001.pdf; Jeremy Freese, Sheri Meland, and William Irwin, "Expressions of Positive Emotion in Photographs, Personality, and Later-Life Marital and Health Outcomes," *Journal of Research in Personality,* 2006, http://www.jeremyfreese .com/docs/FreeseMelandIrwin%20-%20JRP%20-%20ExpressionsPositive EmotionInPhotographs.pdf.

25. Glenn V. Ostir, Kenneth J. Ottenbacher, and Kyriakos S. Markides, "Onset of Frailty in Older Adults and the Protective Role of Positive Affect," *Psychology and Aging* 19 (2004): 402–8.

26. Seligman, *Authentic Happiness*, 40.

27. James Coyne et al., "Emotional Well-Being Does Not Predict Survival in Head and Neck Cancer Patients," *Cancer*, Dec. 1, 2007; Merritt McKinney, "Optimism Doesn't Improve Lung Cancer Survival," *Reuters Health*, Feb. 9, 2004.

28. See, for example, L. B. Kubansky and I. Kawachi, "Going to the Heart of the Matter: Do Negative Emotions Cause Coronary Heart Disease?," *Journal of Psychosomatic Research* 48 (2000): 323–37.

29. Held, "Negative Side of Positive Psychology."

30. Ibid.

31. Melissa Healy, "Truth Is, It's Best If They Know," Oct. 30, 2006, http://www.latimes.com/features/health/la-he-realists30oct30,0,141646.story?coll=la-home-health.

32. Derek M. Isaacowitz, with M. E. P. Seligman, "Is Pessimistic Explanatory Style a Risk Factor for Depressive Mood among Community-Dwelling Older Adults?," *Behaviour Research and Therapy* 39 (2001): 255–72.

33. Mary Duenwald, "Power of Positive Thinking Extends, It Seems, to Aging," *New York Times*, Nov. 19, 2002.

34. Ibid.

35. Quoted in B. Held, "The 'Virtues' of Positive Psychology," *Journal of Theoretical and Philosophical Psychology* 25 (2005): 1–34.

36. Sarah D. Pressman and Sheldon Cohen, "Does Positive Affect Influence Health?" *Psychological Bulletin* 131 (2005): 925–71.

37. http://esi-topics.com/fbp/2007/june07-Pressman_Cohen.html.

38. Seligman, *Authentic Happiness*, 40; Suzanne C. Segerstrom, "Optimism, Goal Conflict, and Stressor-Related Immune Change," *Journal of Behavioral Medicine* 24, no. 5 (2001).

39. Susan Ferraro, "Never a Cloudy Day: The Link between Optimism and Good Health," *New York Daily News*, June 17, 2002.

40. http://www.templeton.org/capabilities_2004/pdf/the_joy_of_giving.pdf.

41. http://latimesblogs.latimes.com/washington/2008/10/a-big-donor-goe.html.

42. John Templeton Foundation, Form 990, 2005.

43. John Templeton Foundation, Capabilities Report, 2006, 77.

44. Freedman, interview with Martin E. P. Seligman.

45. Jane Mayer, "The Experiment: The Military Trains People to Withstand Inter-rogation. Are Those Methods Being Misused at Guantánamo?" *New Yorker,* July 11, 2005, 60.

46. David Montgomery, "A Happiness Gap: Doomacrats and Republigrins," *Washington Post,* Oct. 24, 2008.

47. Daniel Gilbert, *Stumbling on Happiness* (New York: Vintage, 2007), 243.

48. Biswas-Diener and Dean, *Positive Psychology Coaching,* 229.

49. Sam Fulwood III, "Poised for Joy: Life Coaches Teach How to Be Happy," *Cleveland Plain Dealer,* Feb. 9, 2008.

50. Sara Martin, "Seligman Laments People's Tendency to Blame Others," *APA Monitor,* Oct. 1998.

51. Seligman, *Authentic Happiness,* 50.

52. Brad Lemley, "Shiny Happy People: Can You Reach Nirvana with the Aid of Science?" *Discover,* Aug. 2006, http://discovermagazine.com/2006/aug/shiny happy.

53. D. T. Max, "Happiness 101," *New York Times Magazine,* Jan. 7, 2007.

54. http://www.flourishingschools.org/programs.htm.

55. Max, "Happiness 101."

SEVEN. How Positive Thinking Destroyed the Economy

1. Michael A. Fletcher, "1 in 4 Working Families Now Low-Wage, Report Finds," *Washington Post,* Oct. 15, 2008.

2. David Leonhardt, "Larry Summers's Evolution," *New York Times,* June 10, 2007.

3. Leslie Bennetts, "The End of Hubris," *Portfolio,* Dec. 2008, http://www.port folio.com/news-markets/national-news/portfolio/2008/11/19/Greed-and -Doom-on-Wall-Street.

4. John Schmitt and Ben Zipperer, "Is the U.S. a Good Model for Reducing So-cial Exclusion in Europe?," *Center for Economic Policy Review,* Aug. 2006.

5. Carol Graham and Soumya Chattopadhyay, "Gross National Happiness and the Economy," http://www.americanprogress.org/issues/2006/04/b1579981 .html.

6. Dean Baker, *Plunder and Blunder: The Rise and Fall of the Bubble Economy* (Sausalito: Polipoint Press, 2009), 3.

7. Paul Krugman, "Lest We Forget," *New York Times,* Nov. 11, 2008.

8. Quoted in Karen A. Cerulo, *Never Saw It Coming: Cultural Challenges to En-visioning the World* (Chicago: University of Chicago Press, 2006), 61–62.

9. Karin Klein, "Wish for a Cake—and Eat It Too," *Los Angeles Times*, Feb. 13, 2007.

10. Joel Osteen, *Your Best Life Now: 7 Steps to Living at Your Full Potential* (New York: Faith Words, 2004), 7–8.

11. David Van Biema, "Maybe We Should Blame God for the Subprime Mortgage Mess," *Time*, Oct. 3, 2008.

12. Kevin Phillips, *Bad Money: Reckless Finance, Failed Politics, and the Global Crisis of American Capitalism* (New York: Viking, 2008) 92–95.

13. Baker, *Plunder and Blunder*, 97.

14. Stephen S. Roach, "Dying of Consumption," *New York Times*, Nov. 28, 2008; Phillips, *Bad Money*, 43.

15. Alan Zibel, "Personal Bankruptcy Filings Rise 40%," Washingtonpost.com, Jan. 4, 2008.

16. Steven Pearlstein, "A Perfect Storm? No, a Failure of Leadership," *Washington Post*, Dec. 12, 2008.

17. Robert J. Samuelson, "The Engine of Mayhem," *Newsweek*, Oct. 13, 2008, http://www.newsweek.com/id/163743.

18. Steve Fishman, "Burning Down His House," *New York*, Dec. 8, 2008.

19. *Larry King Live*, CNN, Nov. 21, 2008.

20. Jenny Anderson and Vikas Bajaj, "Merrill Tries to Temper the Pollyannas in Its Ranks," *New York Times*, May 15, 2008.

21. http://about.countrywide.com/PressRelease/PressRelease.aspx?rid=515497&pr=yes.

22. Gretchen Morgenson and Geraldine Fabrikant, "Countrywide's Chief Salesman and Defender," *New York Times*, Nov. 11, 2007.

23. Adam Michaelson, *The Foreclosure of America: The Inside Story of the Rise and Fall of Countrywide Home Loans, the Mortgage Crisis, and the Default of the American Dream* (New York: Berkley, 2009), 260, 205, 261.

24. Michael Lewis, "The End of Wall Street's Boom," Portfolio.com, Dec. 2008.

25. Fishman, "Burning Down His House."

26. Jo Becker, Sheryl Gay Stolberg, and Stephen Labaton, "White House Philosophy Stoked Mortgage Bonfire," *New York Times*, Dec. 21, 2008.

27. Julia Hobsbawm, "The Joy of Coaching," May 24, 2007, http://www.spectator.co.uk/the-magazine/business/31040/the-joy-of-coaching.thtml.

28. Baker, *Plunder and Blunder*, 16; Eduardo Porter, "More Than Ever, It Pays to Be the Top Executive," *New York Times*, May 25, 2007.

29. Robert Frank, *Richistan: A Journey through the American Wealth Boom and the Lives of the New Rich* (New York: Crown, 2007), 16.
30. David Lazarus, "Wretched Excess Rides High in Many Executive Suites," *San Francisco Chronicle*, Dec. 29, 2002.
31. http://www.independent.co.uk/news/business/comment/jack-welch-neutron-jack-flattens-the-bleeding-hearts-748440.html.
32. Fishman, "Burning Down His House."
33. Ibid.
34. Eric Dezenhall and John Weber, *Damage Control: How to Get the Upper Hand When Your Business Is under Attack* (New York: Portfolio, 2007), 188.
35. Roger Lowenstein, "Triple-A Failure," *New York Times Magazine*, April 27, 2008.
36. http://marketplace.publicradio.org/display/web/2008/10/23/greenspan/#.
37. Paul Vitello, "An Evangelical Article of Faith: Bad Times Draw Bigger Crowds," *New York Times*, Dec. 14, 2008.
38. *Larry King Live*, CNN, Dec. 8, 2008; "When the Economy Gives You Lemons," *Marketplace*, American Public Media, Nov. 26, 2007.
39. Uri Friedman, "Sales Down, So Firms Boost Morale," *Christian Science Monitor*, Aug. 22, 2008, http://www.csmonitor.com/2008/0822/p03s01-usec.html.
40. Patricia Leigh Brown, "Even if You Can't Buy It, Happiness Is Big Business," *New York Times*, Nov. 27, 2008.
41. Jodie Tillman, "If You're Unhappy and Know It, Shut Up," *St. Petersburg Times*, Jan. 29, 2008.
42. Cindy Krischer Goodman, "How to Survive the Economic Crisis: Be Positive, Proactive," *Miami Herald*, Oct. 28, 2008.
43. Eli Davidson, "How to Get through the Recession with Less Depression," Sept. 25, 2008, http://www.huffingtonpost.com/eli-davidson/how-to-get-through-the-re_b_128971.html.
44. "Tony Robbins, Life Coach, Gives Suggestions for Dealing with Our Shaky Economy," *Today*, MSNBC, Oct. 13, 2008.
45. Dennis Byrne, "Facts You Just Can't Believe In," Dec. 30, 2008, www.chicagotribune.com/news/nationworld/chi-oped1230byrnedec30,0,787857.story.

EIGHT. Postscript on Post–Positive Thinking

1. Sally Quinn and Ben Bradlee, "On Faith: Are You Satisfied with Where You Are Now in Your Life?," *Washington Post*, May 22, 2007, http://www.washingtonpost.com/wp-dyn/content/discussion/2007/05/18/DI2007051801202.html?tid=informbox.

2. Julie K. Norem, *The Positive Power of Negative Thinking: Using Defensive Pessimism to Harness Anxiety and Perform at Your Peak* (New York: Basic, 2001).

3. Atul Gawande, "The Power of Negative Thinking," *New York Times*, May 1, 2007.

4. Ryszard Kapuscinski, *Shah of Shahs* (New York: Vintage, 1992), 89.

5. Dubravka Ugresic, *Thank You for Not Reading* (Chicago: Dalkey Archive, 2003), 86.

6. Pekka Pesonen, "Utopias to Norms: From Classicism to Socialist Realism," http://www.slav.helsinki.fi/studies/huttunen/mosaiikki/retro/en/centre-periphery/pp2_eng.htm.

7. Ugresic, *Thank You*, 86.

8. John Marks Templeton, *The Templeton Plan: 21 Steps to Personal Success and Real Happiness* (West Conshohocken: Templeton Foundation, 1997), 118.

9. Carlin Flora, "The Pursuit of Happiness," http://www.psychologytoday.com/articles/index.php?term=pto-4738.html&fromMod=emailed.

10. Donald Meyer, *The Positive Thinkers: Popular Religious Psychology from Mary Baker Eddy to Norman Vincent Peale and Ronald Reagan* (Middletown: Wesleyan University Press, 1998), 393.

11. Victoria Moore, "Promising You Can Have Anything Just by Thinking about It, It's No Surprise *The Secret* Has Become the Fastest-Selling Self-Help Book Ever," *Daily Mail* (London), April 26, 2007.

12. "Psychologist Produces the First-Ever 'World Map of Happiness,'" *Science-Daily*, Nov. 14, 2006, http://www.sciencedaily.com/releases/2006/11/061113093726.htm.

13. David Leonhardt, "Money Doesn't Buy Happiness. Well, on Second Thought . . ." *New York Times*, April 16, 2008.

14. Fernanda Santos, "Are New Yorkers Happy? Some More Than Others," *New York Times*, March 8, 2009.

Acknowledgments

Book writing can be a lonely business, but in this case I was able to pull together a little support group of people who were also challenging the prevailing positive-thinking consensus: Barbara Held, Jim Coyne, Micki McGee, Heather Love, Richard P. Sloan, and, most recently, Karen Cerulo. We conferred at length by phone, e-mail, and at our jolly annual "negative lunches," and I thank them all for sharing their ideas and keeping me up to date—especially Barbara Held and Jim Coyne, who took the time to read and comment on chapter drafts.

If he had lived long enough, historian Donald Meyer would have been a perfect addition to this group. I returned to his brilliant book *The Positive Thinkers: Popular Religious Psychology from Mary Baker Eddy to Norman Vincent Peale and Ronald Reagan* again and again while working on mine.

Others who were dragooned into reading and commenting on chapters include Bob Richardson, Ben Ehrenreich, Robert Orsi,

Steve Eisman, Gary Long, and the delightful Eric Dezenhall. I also thank the many people who took time to talk or correspond with me along the way, including Catherine Albanese, Rosa Brooks, James Champy, David Collins, Aine Donovan, Marla Frederick, Carol Graham, Jonathan Haidt, Arlie Hochschild, Robert Jackall, Janet McIntosh, Helen Meldrum, Tom Morris, Nomi Prins, Ashley Pinnington, Vickie Sullivan, Howard Tennen, and Neil Weinstein. Sanho Tree and Tim Townsend shared their research on the Templeton Foundation with me; Diane Alexander provided invaluable assistance at many stages in the process.

Kris Dahl was more than the agent for this book; she was a source of important contacts and insights. Much thanks to Riva Hocherman for her insightful suggestions and to Roslyn Schloss for her expert copyediting. And there's no adequate way to thank my editor, Sara Bershtel, whose humanism and laserlike logic inform every line of this book.

Index

About the Author

———

BARBARA EHRENREICH is the author of sixteen books, including *Dancing in the Streets* and the *New York Times* bestsellers *Nickel and Dimed* and *Bait and Switch*. A frequent contributor to *Harper's* and the *Nation*, she has also been a columnist at the *New York Times* and *Time* magazine.

She can be reached at www.barbaraehrenreich.com.